AF644492

A New Curve in the Ganges
Mahatma Gandhi's Interpretation of Hinduism

A New Curve in the Ganges
Mahatma Gandhi's Interpretation of Hinduism

by
Arvind Sharma
Faculty of Religious Studies
McGill University

D.K.Printworld (P) Ltd.
New Delhi

Cataloging in Publication Data — DK
[courtesy: D.K. Agencies (P) Ltd.<docinfo@dkagencies.com>]

Sharma, Arvind, 1940 –
A new curve in the Ganges: Mahatma Gandhi's interpretation of Hinduism / by Arvind Sharma.
p. 23 cm.
Includes bibliographical references (p.)
Includes index.
ISBN 8124602719

1. Gandhi, Mahatma, 1869-1948. -- Religion. 2. Hinduism. 1. Title.

DDC 294.5 21

ISBN 81-246-0271-9
First Published in India in 2005
©Author

All rights reserved. No part of this publication may be reproduced or transmitted in any form or by any means, electronic or mechanical, including photocopying, recording, or any information storage or retrieval system, without prior written permission of both the copyright owner, indicated above, and the publisher.

Published and printed by:
D.K. Printworld (P) Ltd.
Regd. office : '*Sri Kunj*', F-52, Bali Nagar
New Delhi - 110 015
Phones : (011) 2545-3975; 2546-6019; *Fax* : (011) 2546-5926
E-mail: dkprintworld@vsnl.net
Web: www.dkprintworld.com

Contents

Introduction

The mystique which surrounds the name of Mahatma Gandhi is more calculated to evoke admiration than promote analysis. And even though more than half a century has elapsed since he made his sublime departure from our midst with the name of Rāma on his lips, during the course of which attempts have been made to demythologize him in various ways, his charisma still seems to rise above the miasma of confusion generated by these critiques. In a sense the greatness of such a person transcends any individual discussion of his particular failures and successes.

Difficult as it might be to be analytical about such a charismatic figure as Mahatma Gandhi, specially when one is analyzing his relationship with such a protean tradition as the Hindu, such an analysis is definitely worth undertaking because Mahatma Gandhi wrestled with his tradition instead of merely following it, implying thereby that wrestling with one's religious tradition might well be the most faithful way of following it. This book is an attempt to analyze this curious relationship.

Mahatma Gandhi stands in a special relationship with Hinduism, a relationship rich in ironies. Himself excommunicated by his caste on his return from England, he fought all his life for the rights of the Untouchables — the permanently excommunicated within it as it were; an avid reader of the *Bhagavad-Gītā* which he interpreted allegorically, he was assassinated by another avid reader of the *Bhagavad-Gītā* who took it literally. He claimed to be a Sanātanī Hindu, a Hindu of the deepest dye, but he had passages from virtually all the religions of the world read at his prayer-meetings. Yet these are small ironies compared to the fact that in the very process of following his religion, which he claimed was Hinduism, he transformed it.

This book sets out to examine whether any pattern underlies his versatile engagement with his own tradition. Should it be possible to identify a pattern, however, it will come at a price. That price is precision. One loses in precision what one gains in pattern. It is for the reader to decide after he or she has read this book whether the price was worth it.

1

Mahatma Gandhi and the Sources of Dharma in Hinduism

Mahatma Gandhi and the Hindu religion constitute the two Archimedean points,[1] so to say, of this monograph. When a relationship between two points of reference is being inquired into, it makes sense to begin by asking what these points of reference are. In the context of this monograph such a procedure is bound to raise two questions: who is Mahatma Gandhi[2] and what is the

1. J.G. Arapura, *Religion as Anxiety and Tranquility* (The Hague: Mouton, 1972), pp. 38-39, 50.

2. For Mahatma Gandhi's self-disclosure on the question, see M.K. Gandhi, *The Story of My Experiments with Truth* (Washington, D.C.: Public Affairs Press, 1948). For a biographical account approved by Mahatma Gandhi himself, see D.G. Tendulkar, *Mahatma: Life of Mohandas Karamchand Gandhi* (8 volumes; Bombay: Vithalbhai K. Jhaveri and D.G. Tendulkar, 1951). "There are at present about four hundred biographies of Gandhi" (Ved Mehta, *New Yorker*, May 10, 1976, p. 43). For capsulized accounts of his life and deeds see Gandhi, Mohandas Karamchand, in *Chamber's Encyclopaedia* (new revised edition, Oxford: Pergamon Press Ltd., 1966), vol. VI, pp. 153-54; Gandhi, Mohandas Karamchand (Mahatma), in *Collier's*

Hindu religion?[3]

Encyclopaedia (U.S.A.: Crowell Collier and Macmillan Inc., 1966), vol. 10, pp. 564-65; Gandhi, Mohandas Karamchand, in *Everyman's Encyclopaedia*, 4th edn. (London: J.M. Dent & Sons Ltd., 1958) vol. 5, pp. 604-05; Gandhi, Mohandas Karamchand, in *Funk & Wagnalls Standard Reference Encyclopaedia* (New York: Standard Reference Works Publishing Company Inc., 1959), vol. II, pp. 3895-98; Gandhi, Mohandas Karamchand, in *Encyclopaedia Americana*, international edn. (New York: Americana Corporation, 1965), vol. 12, pp. 271-72; Gandhi, Mohandas Karamchand, in *Encyclopaedia Britannica* (U.S.A.: Encyclopaedia Britannica Inc., 1968), vol. 9, pp. 1128-31; Gandhi, Mahatma, in *The New Encyclopaedia Britannica*, Macropaedia, 15th edn. (Chicago: Encyclopaedia Britannica Inc., 1974), vol. 19, pp. 648-52, Bart Gruzalski, *On Gandhi* (Belmont, CA: Wadsworth/Thompson Learning Inc., 2001), etc.

3. The question has been answered variously or not at all; sometimes its very legitimacy has been questioned; see Whitfield Foy, ed., *Man's Religious Quest* (London: Croon Helm, 1978), pp. 49-50. Also see *The New Encyclopaedia Britannica*, vol. 8, pp. 889-99; M.N. Srinivas and A.M. Shah, "Hinduism," in David L. Sills, ed., *International Encyclopaedia of the Social Sciences* (The Macmillan Co. and the Free Press, 1968), p. 358; M.N. Srinivas, "Hinduism," in *Encyclopaedia Britannica*, vol. 10 (Chicago: William Benton, 1961), p. 575; A.L. Basham, "Hinduism," in *Encyclopaedia Britannica*, vol. 11 (Chicago: William Benton, 1968), p. 507; Roderick Marshall, "Hinduism," in *Encyclopaedia Americana* (New York: Americana Corporation, 1965), p. 198b; Ninian Smart, "Hinduism," in S.G.F. Brandon, ed., *A Dictionary of Comparative Religion* (New York: Charles Scribner's Sons, 1970), p. 331; Joseph W. Elder, "Hinduism," in *Collier's Encyclopaedia* (Cromwell, Collier and Macmillan Inc., 1966),

Although the life and deeds of Mahatma Gandhi may remain forever a subject of investigation[4] and perhaps even

---

p. 127; H. Julius Eggling, "Hinduism," in *Encyclopaedia Britannica* (Chicago: Encyclopaedia Britannica Ltd., 1951), p. 577; A.C. Bouquet, "Hinduism," in *Chambers Encyclopaedia*, vol. VII (New York: Oxford University Press, 1950), pp. 97-98; W. Crooke, "Hinduism," in James Hastings, ed., *Encyclopaedia of Religion and Ethics* (New York: Charles Scribner's Sons, 1919), pp. 712-13; William Bridgewater and Seymour Kurtz, eds., *The Columbia Encyclopaedia* (New York: Columbia University Press, 1950), p. 951; etc. Also see Gunther D. Sontheimer and Hermann Kulke, eds., *Hinduism Reconsidered* (New Delhi: Manohar, 1989).

4. This can be easily seen from the bibliographic enterprise which has become a part of Gandhiana (see Ved Mehta, *op. cit.*, p. 75 ff). "There are two standard bibliographies of Gandhian literature: 'Mahatma Gandhi: A Descriptive Bibliography' by Jagdish Sharma, which was first published in 1955 and was brought out in a second edition in 1968, and 'Gandhi Bibliography,' by Dharma Vir, which was published in 1967" (*ibid.*, p. 86). A more recent one is *Mohandas Karmachand Gandhi: A Bibliography* (New Delhi: Orient Longman, 1974). For a review see S.R. Tikekar, "Bibliography or technophilia?" in *Gandhi Marg* 21 (4), 290-94.

5. Many biographies on the Mahatma, like those on other saintly figures, end up by becoming hagiographies. The point of interest to the student of religion, however, is the fact that Mahatma Gandhi is coming to be depicted, in popular Hindu literature, as an incarnation of God. As Milton Singer points out (Milton Singer, ed., *Traditional India: Structure and Change* [Philadelphia: The American Folklore Society, 1959], p. 158):

of sublime speculation,[5] for the purposes of this paper the

---

> Several *harikathās* about Gandhi's life have been written and performed. One of these was recorded by another lady *bhāgavatar* who comes from a Brahman Vaisnava family in Mysore. On her version the story of Gandhi's life is told after the fashion of the lives of the saints. In fact, Gandhi is treated as an incarnation (*avatāra*) of God who has come to deliver India from foreign domination. Gandhi's death is also effectively told as the death of a martyr. Gandhi Bhāgavatar (Rājārām), a Tamil Smārta Brahman and a Tamil poet was a pioneer in this line.
>
> To tell Gandhi's story the reciter uses all the songs and Sanskrit verses that are used in the traditional *harikathā*. She begins with the famous song of the Gujarati saint Narasimha Mehta, which starts with the words, "Vaiṣṇava janato," and declares that "he is a true devotee of Lord Viṣṇu who knows the suffering of others." This was Gandhi's favorite song. The reciter emphasizes the great faith which Gandhi had in devotion (*bhakti*) and in the recital of Rama's name. Gandhi's doctrine of help and uplift for the poor and his belief in equality are also stressed.

This may represent the culmination of a tendency already present in Mahatma Gandhi's lifetime for "There is evidence that (whether seriously or in mere adulation) King George V and Mahatma Gandhi have both in their day been addressed as Raghubansmani, an epithet which properly belongs to *avatar*s of Vishnu" (A.C. Bouquet, *Hinduism* [New York: Hutchinson's University Library, 1948], p. 92).

recognition of Mahatma Gandhi as a person, as an identifiable individual who was born in 1869 in Porbandar and died in 1948 in New Delhi would seem to suffice at this stage.[6] It is rather the other question: what is the Hindu religion? — which appears to be the more formidable of the two. Indeed, before one may speak of the Hindu religion one may well ask: what do Hindus mean by religion?

> What then does an Indian think of when one speaks of religion? The word that most nearly corresponds to "religion" in its meaning is *yoga*, which means "uniting." The word *yoga* and the English word "yoke" have the same Indo-Germanic root (*yuj*), meaning "to join." *Yoga* has, therefore, come to mean the practice — bodily and mental — that leads to our joining the origin of our being. Although this word corresponds to "religion" in its general meaning, it is not used in India to mean religion. The word often used for religion is *dharma*. *Dharma* is etymologically what sustains, supports. It is what supports life, and life is sustained only when it is not in discord with its basis, the origin of our being. *Dharma* has, therefore, come to mean the law, and then the law of life. Existence depends upon the laws of its being. If they are violated, existence becomes non-existence.

---

6. For such purposes Louis Fischer's *The Life of Mahatma Gandhi* (New York: Harper & Brothers, 1950) seems quite adequate.

> *Dharma* is therefore the law of life, the way of life, that keeps it running in union with the foundations of our being. In this sense, *Dharma* is a way of life in accord with reality. We can speak of the Cārvāka-*dharma* also, although the Cārvāka teaching is thoroughly materia-listic and atheistic, and does not believe in the reality of any spirit and any objective validity even of ethical laws.
>
> The Indians have used the word *mata* also for religion. We can speak of Christian *mata* and Islamic *mata*, just as we speak of Christian *dharma* and Islamic *dharma*. But *mata* means, as mentioned above, opinion, doctrine, theory, view. So the Indian regards religion as a theory of reality guiding our life and also as a way or plan of life according to that theory.[7]

What the Hindus mean by religion then, is *dharma*.[8] Indeed as has been pointed out:

> Indians themselves, if they belong to the

7. P.T. Raju, *The Philosophical Traditions of India* (University of Pittsburgh Press, 1971) pp. 26-27; also see Charles A. Moore, ed., *The Indian Mind* (Honolulu: University of Hawaii Press, 1967), p. 184. For the evolution of the meaning of *dharma* and its various senses see P.V. Kane, *History of Dharmaśāstra*, vol. I, part I (Poona: Bandarkar Oriental Research Institute, 1968), pp. 1-6.

8. "*Dharma* means 'law' or 'sacred law' in Hindu tradition and can be used for 'religion': Hindu religion is the *sanatana dharma* or 'everlasting law'" (S.G.F. Brandon, ed., *op. cit.*, p. 236).

Hindu tradition, have a variety of ways of referring to it. One classical expression is *arya dharma*, the noble order, or noble law; another is *sanatana dharma*, or eternal law; a third is *Hindu dharma*, which we can only translate as Indian law or Hindu law. What these all have in common is the word *dharma*, which means a variety of things, but which may perhaps be summed up as the sacred order, or law. *Dharma* is both the way things are and the way they should be, the only appropriate order for the universe and for man in it. This includes the various manifestations of what we call religion: ritual, devotion, myth and doctrine; it also includes social order (as *varnashramadharma*, the caste system as a form of sacred law) and philosophical theories of man and the universe. Like all laws, *dharma* may be observed, or it may not; but whether or not it has followers, it will remain inviolate and inviolable.

From the Hindu point of view, then, there is a strong *prima facie* case of avoiding the term "Hinduism" altogether and using instead *Hindu dharma* or some such expression more in line with Hindu usage. But the term "Hinduism" has become too deeply entrenched in Western vocabulary to be easily dislodged. Moreover, it is now widely used by Hindus themselves whenever they have to express themselves in English. For instance, the first chapter in Morgan's book "The Religion of the Hindus," written by the leading Indian historian is called "The Nature and History of Hinduism."[9]

---

9. John R. Hinnells and Eric J. Sharpe, *Hinduism* (Newcastle upon Tyne: Oriel Press, 1972), p. 2. The uneasiness of scholars with the use of the term Hinduism has been remarked upon by the authors earlier when they wrote: "The Western student approaching Hinduism for the first time is faced with what may seem to be insurmountable obstacles to understanding. Not the least of these is the question of definition. What exactly *is* Hinduism? Is it a religion, or many religions and many philosophies? Certainly it is kaleidoscopic in its variety, and a slight change of approach or emphasis may well give the observer the impression that all its elements have shifted — some merging into others, others again standing out with renewed colour and clarity. The historian sees one thing, the mystic another, the sociologist something quite different.

Perhaps, therefore, the first question which we ought to ask is whether the single English word "Hinduism" is at all appropriate to describe the phenomenon we are trying to study. It is not merely a matter of diversity. Christianity, Islam and Buddhism are also very diverse religions; but in these cases the problem may in part be resolved by making references to the teachings of the founder and to the beliefs and practices of a historic community of believers. Judaism is capable of fairly close definition on similar lines, through Moses, the Law, the Prophets and the community. However, in the case of Hinduism this approach simply will not work. It is not a "founded" religion. It has no creeds — except in some unusual cases, and these are as a rule accepted only within the group which has produced them. Its holy scriptures are of immense size and staggering diversity. It has nothing even remotely approaching a central

Mahatma Gandhi himself used the term Hinduism freely, but it is also clear that he understood the term Hinduism to mean the Hindu religion, that is, the religion of the Hindus

---

organization (or ecclesiastical authority), and would not know what do with it if it had one. In short, whatever it is, and whatever is unity, that unity is neither doctrinal nor organizational. Not surprisingly, then, one modern Western observer, whose opinions must always be treated with respect, has written that "The term 'Hinduism' is . . . a particularly false conceptualization, one that is conspicuously incompatible with any adequate understanding of the religious outlook of Hindus."

The state by which this term came into popular use in the West to describe the traditional religion of India are interesting, but we cannot go into them now. It is worth mentioning, however, that the words "Hindu" and "Hinduism" are basically geographical, derived, *via* Persian, from the name of that river now called Indus. A "Hindu" was originally a dweller in the land of the Indus who did not happen to have made his submission to Islam (and this of course dates to the Middle Ages). Hindu*ism,* then — Europeans love "isms" — is the European blanket term which is used to cover the religion of all those Indians who do not happen to be Muslims, Christians, Parsis, Jains or Buddhists. In other words, it is a term originally applied by those who are not members of this particular tradition (or these particular traditions) to those who are. It would not be surprising to find that it had loopholes and shortcomings" (*ibid.*, pp. 1, 2). Also see Arvind Sharma, ed., *The Study of Hinduism* (Columbia, South Carolina: University of South Carolina Press, 2003) Chapter One.

and by the term religion he meant *dharma*.[10] As for the term Hindu he repeats the usual explanation of the origin of the term.[11]

Now *dharma* in Hinduism is generally regarded as

---

10. Sometimes, however, Mahatma Gandhi seems to use the term in the sense of ideal religion, as in M.K. Gandhi, *Hindu Dharma* (Ahmedabad: Navajivan Publishing House, 1958), p. 11. Elsewhere Mahatma Gandhi also equates the word *dharma* with faith (*ibid.*, p. 8).

11. "[Referring to a question that was sent by a member of the audience, What is a Hindu? What is the origin of the word? Is there any Hinduism? Gandhiji said:] These were pertinent questions for the time. He was no historian, he laid claim to no learning. But he did read in some authentic book on Hinduism that the word *Hindu* did not occur in the Vedas but when Alexander the Great invaded India, the inhabitants of the country to the east of the Sindhu, which is known by the English-speaking Indians as the Indus, were described as Hindus. The letter *S* had become *H* in Greek. The religion of these inhabitants became Hinduism and they know it, it was a most tolerant religion. It gave shelter to the early Christians who had fled from persecution, also to the Jews known as Beni-Israel as also to the Parsis. He was proud to belong to that Hinduism which was all-inclusive, and which stood for tolerance. Aryan scholars swore by what they called the *Vedic* religion and Hindustan was otherwise known as Aryavarta. He had no such aspiration." (Hindu Dharma, p. 229). For a recent discussion of the word and associated terms see Arvind Sharma, "On Hindu, Hindustan, Hinduism and Hindutva," *Numen* 49:1-36 (2002).

growing from four "roots,"[12] or as flowing from four sources. Thus

> Manu-samhita says there are four sources of morality (*dharma*): the Vedas (the scriptures), the Smrti literature based on these, the conduct of good and wise persons, and the individual's own judgement.[13]

What is not immediately obvious from this listing[14] is that the order of the enumeration of the four sources mentioned

---

12. *Manu-Smṛti* II.12; *Yājñavalkya-Smṛti* I.7; also see *Āpastamba Dharma-Sūtra* I, 1, 1, 1-3; *Gautama Dharma-Sūtra* I, 1-4; *Vasiṣṭha Dharma-Sūtra* I.4-6; etc. G. Bühler (*The Laws of Manu* [Delhi: Motilal Banarsidass, 1964 [first published 1886], p. 30) translates the text of Manu thus:

    > 6. The whole Veda is the (first) source of the sacred law, next the tradition and the virtuous conduct of those who know (the Veda further), also the customs of holy men, and (finally) self-satisfaction.

13. Charles A. Moore, ed., *op. cit.*, p. 344. The relevant verses are cited as II.1, 6, 12 (*ibid.*, p. 357). P.V. Kane, however, offers a slightly different interpretation of the text: "The Manusmṛti lays down five different sources of *dharma*, the whole Veda is (the foremost) source of *dharma* and (next) the tradition and the practice of those who know it (the Veda), and further the usages of virtuous men and self-satisfaction" (*op. cit.*, vol. I, p. 6; emphasis added).

14. See. G. Bühler, *op. cit.*, p. 30. "There are, according to Manu, four ways of determining right and wrong. Veda, *smṛti, ācāra* (good conduct), and conscience. While the former three make for social order, social progress is achieved by the last. We

above is important. If these four sources are generally rendered as:

1. Revelation;[15]
2. Tradition;[16]
3. Exemplary conduct;[17]
4. Conscience;[18]

then the order of the enumeration implies that the former source(s) take precedence over the later ones.[19]

---

should do what appeals to our conscience (*ātmanaḥ priyam*) (II.12)" (Sarvepalli Radhakrishnan and Charles A. Moore, ed., *A Source Book in Indian Philosophy* [Princeton University Press, 1957], p. 172). These remarks seem to obscure the fact that the order of enumeration is significant and emphasize the role of conscience, examples of which are not wanting in Indian literature (see *Abhijñāna-Śākuntalam,* I.22) but the current emphasis on which seems to be modern.

15. T.M.P. Mahadevan, *Outlines of Hinduism* (Bombay: Chetana Ltd., 1960), p. 28.

16. *Ibid.*

17. For a more technical sense of the term *ācāra* as distinguished from *vyavahāra* see Vaman Shivram Apte, *The Practical Sanskrit-English Dictionary* (Delhi: Motilal Banarsidass, 1965), p. 205. Also see Benjamin Walker, *The Hindu World,* vol. I (New York: Frederick A. Praeger, 1968), p. 588.

18. For "self-satisfaction," see G. Bühler, *op. cit.*, p. 30.

19. It is useful in this context to offer a purely traditional explanation of the four sources of their relationship, in contrast with the modern, as has been done by Ganganath Jha (*Manu-Smriti Notes,* Part II [University of Calcutta, 1924], pp. 39-40): "'Vedah' is the collection of Mantra and

What Mahatma Gandhi did, in effect, was to reverse the order. Thus, while revelation or *śruti* is *dharma* heard

---

Brahmana texts, as defined by Āpastamba; — *'akhilah'*, the actual texts available, as also those presumed on the strength of 'Transference' and that of 'Indicative Power,' 'Syntactical Connection,' 'Contest,' 'Position' and 'Name' (Jaimini iii); - or *'akhilah,'* 'entire,' may be taken as meant to preclude the notion that the said authority belongs only to the three Vedas, and *not* to the 'Atharva', which is based upon such assertions of Āpastamba and others as 'Yajña is enjoined by the *three* Vedas.' That the 'Atharva is an authority for Dharma is due to the fact that it prescribes the performance of the *Tulā-puruṣa* and other propitiatory rites for all castes, even though it does not deal mainly with the performance of the Agnihotra or other *Śrauta* rites. — When the text says that these are the means of known *'Dharma,' right,* it implies that they are the means of knowing also what is *'Adharma,' 'wrong,'* it being necessary for the scriptures to furnish an idea of all that is wrong and hence a source of impurity of the mind, which obstructs the acquiring of true knowledge. — *'Mūlam,'* 'Source,' the means of knowing. — *'Tadvidām,'* those learned in the Veda; this implies that in the case of *'Smṛti'* and the rest, the authority is not inherent in themselves, but due to their being based upon the Veda. — *'Smṛti,'* the *Dharmaśāstra* compiled by Yājñavalkya and others. — *'Śīla'* implies the thirteen qualities enumerated by Hārīta — *viz.,* Faith in Brahman, Devotion to Gods and *Pitṛs*, Gentility, Harmlessness, Freedom from jealousy, Freedom from harshness, Friendliness, Sweetness of speech, Gratefulness, Kindness for sufferers, Sympathy, Calmness. This *'Śīla'* differs from *Ācāra*; it stands for the negative virtues, the *avoidance of wrong,* while the former stands for the positive active virtues; the doing of right. — *'Ācāra,'* the tying of the bracelet during marriage and so forth. — *'Sādhūnām*

from without,[20] according to Mahatma Gandhi "Our

ātmanastuṣṭiḥ,' whenever doubt arises regarding what is right, what determines the question is the 'self-satisfaction' of those that are *'Sādhu,' i.e.,* have their minds replete with the knowledge of the Veda and the impressions gathered therefrom; *i.e.,* that course is to be accepted as 'right,' which commands the unanimous approval of the said persons; — such is the explanation suggested by the *Kalpataru.* In support of this view we have the following passage from the *Taittirīya,* relating to cases of doubt regarding *Dharma,* — 'Thou shouldst behave in a manner in which behave those Brahmanas who are impartial, honest, steady, calm and righteous.' This implies the authority of the Pariṣad 'Assembly.' — Or *'sādhūnām'* may be construed with *'āchāraḥ,'* which would imply the authority also of those 'good men' — men free from all evil qualities, — who are not 'learned in the Veda;' so that for superior *Śūdras*, the practices of their forefathers would be authoritative. — 'Self-satisfaction' is the determining factor in the case of options; but this is an authority for the man himself, not for others."

20. The Vedas are the ultimate source of *dharma* and although it is commonly asserted that the "ṛṣis *saw* the truths or *heard* them" (T.M.P. Mahadevan, *op. cit.*, p. 29, emphasis added) the exact mode of their reception is not entirely clear. According to the Nyāya tradition, God is the author of the Vedas and they are revealed to the sages at the beginning of each aeon. The exact mode of revelation is however far from clear (see K. Satchidananda Murty, *Revelation and Reason in Advaita Vedānta* [New York: Columbia University Press, 1959], p. 223 ff). In the case of the Mīmāṁsā school it is clear that the mode of revelation is usually believed to be verbal (see Haridas Bhattacharyya, ed., *The Cultural Heritage of India* III [Calcutta: the Ramakrishna Mission, 1953], p. 151ff). In

religion has its source from God within."[21] As Bhataran Kumarappa points out,

> He would not allow the scriptures to stifle man's conscience. His ultimate appeal was always to the still small voice within, even if its verdict was in conflict with the *shastras*, so long as it was in conformity with truth and

---

the case of Advaita Vedanta, it is possible to argue that the Vedas are revealed through internal inspiration, as K. Satchidananda Murty points out (*op. cit.*, p. 50): "Śaṅkara quotes a *Ṛg-Vedic* passage which says that the sacrificers qualified themselves to receive the Veda by performing sacrifices, and later obtained the Word, which was in possession of the sages. According to him, sages and gods who excel in knowledge and action by virtue of their actions in the past aeon, are able to recollect the Veda by God's grace as it was in the past aeon, just as a man waking from sleep is able to recollect and continue his previous waking experience. He also quotes with approval a *smṛti* text which says that Śaunaka and Madhucchandas were enabled to 'see' the Vedic texts. Such passages from Śaṅkara would imply that according to him, God makes the Vedic propositions flash in the minds of the sages in the same linguistic form in which they are now available. Hence in the sacredness of Veda, its verbal inerrancy and the caution that change or mispronunciation of even a single letter will break one's head."

It may be noted, however, that the Vedas, even if heard as the voice in the heart, do not constitute the voice of conscience, which Mahatma Gandhi emphasized.

21. M.K. Gandhi, *Hindu Dharma*, p. 305.

non-violence.[22]

During the course of a conversation with Mr. Basil Mathews, Mahatma Gandhi was asked point blank: "Where do you find the seat of authority?" Gandhi replied:

> It lies here (pointing to his breast). I exercise my judgement about every scripture, including the *Gita*. I cannot let a scriptural text supersede my reason. Whilst I believe that the principal books are inspired, they suffer from a process of double distillation. Firstly, they come through a human prophet, and then through the commentaries of interpreters. Nothing in them comes from God directly. Matthew may give one version of one text, and John may give another. I cannot surrender my reason whilst I subscribe to divine revelation. And above all, "the letter killeth, the spirit giveth life." But you must not misunderstand my position. I believe in Faith also, in things where Reason has no place, e.g., the existence of God. No argument can move me from that faith, and like that little girl who repeated against all reason "yet we are seven," I would like to repeat, on being baffled in argument by a very superior intellect, "Yet there is a God."[23]

22. M.K. Gandhi, *Hindu Dharma*, p. vi.
23. *Ibid.*, p. 34. For a discussion of the *dharma* and its sources from a legal rather than an ethical point of view in a modern context see K.B. Panda, *Sanatan Dharma and Law* (Cuttack: Sm. Sushila Panda, 1974).

The importance of proper conduct based on a conscience sensitive to truth and non-violence can hardly be underrated in the Gandhian scheme. The importance he attached to *ācāra*[24] manifested itself in several ways. He himself practised non-violence to such an extent that he could be proclaimed its *ācārya*; even otherwise he remarked that:

> *Charya* means course of conduct; *brahma-charya* conduct adapted to the search of Brahma, i.e., Truth. From this etymological meaning arises the special meaning, viz., control of all the senses.[25]

It is a point of considerable interest in this context that Mahatma Gandhi should appeal to the Hindu epics and the *Gītā* — or Smṛti literature in the broader sense much more than to the Vedas.[26] "Nothing elates me so much as

---

24. See Monier Monier-Williams, *A Sanskrit-English Dictionary* (Oxford: Clarendon Press, 1976), p. 131. J. Gonda seems to miss the point of the distinction between *guru* and an *ācārya* from this point of view (see *Change and Continuity in Indian Religion* [The Hague: Mouton, 1965], p. 26 ff).
25. M.K. Gandhi, *Hindu Dharma*, p. 227.
26. The following remarks by T.M.P. Mahadevan are not out of place here: "For a long time in the history of Hinduism it was considered a sacrilege to write a religious or philosophical work in any of the popular languages of India. But, if the truths of religion and philosophy are to be brought home to the mind of the commoner, Sanskrit which is a difficult tongue to learn, requiring considerable effort and application, will not be of much avail. Even from the earliest times we find the protest movements making use of the local

the music of the *Gita* or the *Ramayana* of Tulsidas, the only two books in Hinduism I may be said to know."[27] As an argument against the practice of untouchability he cited the attitude of Rāma towards Śabarī[28] and pointed out that:

dialects for purposes of propagating their views. The early Buddhist literature is in Pali. The Jainas wrote their early books in Ardhamagadhi. But these two schools soon realised that they would not gain philosophical recognition if their thoughts were not dressed in Sanskrit, with the result that the later works of these schools came to be written in that language. But with the march of time this attitude changed, and we have today a mass of philosophical and religious literature in each of the popular languages. To instance but a few, the *Tēvāram* and the *Tiruvācakam* are well-known among the hymns of the Śaiva saints of South India; the Vaiṣṇavas have correspondingly the *Divya-prabandham* and other devotional songs; the Caitanya movement and the songs of Tagore are responsible for the enrichment of Bengali devotional literature; the songs of Kabīr, the *Abhaṅga*s of the Mahārāṣṭra saints, the *Rāmāyaṇa* of Tulsī Dās are all outpourings of God-intoxicated souls. If the essentials of Hinduism have found a place, difficult to dislodge, in the homes of even the lowliest and the last in this vast country, it is not a little due to these devotional poems in the languages of the people. To all of them the name 'Veda' may be given, for has not the Veda itself declared that the Vedas are many, unending (*anantā vai vedāḥ*)?" (*op. cit.*, pp. 38-39).

27. M.K. Gandhi, *Hindu Dharma*, p. 7.

28. Interestingly he rejected "The story of a *shudra* having been punished by Ramachandra for daring to learn the Vedas . . . as an interpolation" (M.K. Gandhi, *Hindu Dharma*, p. 9). The ghost of Sambuka, however, is not so easily exorcised and will re-appear later.

> Lord Krishna has also taught that to be a true *bhakta* we should make no difference between a *brahmana* and a scavenger.[29]

Vedic authority, the ultimate touchstone of *dharma* in traditional Hinduism, was to the Mahatma nothing more than a mere stone until it possessed the magic touch of actual spiritual living.[30]

At this point it could be argued that Mahatma Gandhi called himself "a *Sanatani* Hindu because (1) I believe in the Vedas, the Upanishads, the Puranas and all that goes by the name of Hindu scriptures. . . ."[31] It should, however, be

---

29. M.K. Gandhi, *Hindu Dharma*, p. 139.

30. "Mere knowledge of the Vedas cannot make our *brahmans* spiritual preceptors. If it did Max-Müller would have been one" (M.K. Gandhi, *Hindu Dharma*, p. 11). "The Vedas represent the truth, they are infinite. But who has known them in their entirety? What goes today by the name of Vedas are not even a millionth part of the real Veda — the Book of Knowledge. And who knows the entire meaning of even the few books that we have? Rather than wade through these infinite complications, our sages taught us to learn one thing: 'As with the Self, so with the Universe.' It is not possible to scan the universe, as it is to scan the self. Know the self and you know the universe. But even knowledge of the self within presupposes ceaseless striving — not only ceaseless but pure, and the pure striving presupposes a pure heart, which in turn depends on the practice of *yamas* and *niyamas* — the *cardinal* and *casual* virtues." (*ibid.*, p. 20).

31. M.K. Gandhi, *Hindu Dharma*, p. 6; also quoted in T.M.P. Mahadevan, *op. cit.*, p. 287.

noted that immediately after stating the other three conditions on the basis of which Mahatma Gandhi claimed to be Sanātanī Hindu, he wrote:

> The reader will note that I have purposely refrained from using the word divine origin in reference to the Vedas or any other scriptures. For I do not believe in the exclusive divinity of the Vedas. I believe the Bible, the Quran, and the Zend Avesta to be as much divinely inspired as the Vedas. My belief in the Hindu scriptures does not require me to accept every word and every verse as divinely inspired. Nor do I claim to have any first-hand knowledge of these wonderful books. But I do claim to know and feel the truths of the essential teaching of the scriptures. I decline to be bound by any interpretation, however learned it may be, if it is repugnant to reason or moral sense. I do most emphatically repudiate the claim (if they advance as such) of the present *Shankaracarya*s and *shastri*s to give a correct interpretation of the Hindu scriptures. On the contrary I believe that our present knowledge of these books is in a most chaotic state. I believe implicitly in the Hindu aphorism, that no one truly knows the *shastra*s who has not attained perfection in Innocence (*ahimsa*), Truth (*satya*) and Self-control (*brahmacharya*) and who has not renounced all acquisition or possession of wealth. I believe in the institution of *guru*s, but in this age millions must go without a *guru*, because it is a rare thing to find a combination of perfect

> purity and perfect learning. But one need not despair of ever knowing the truth of one's religion, because the fundamentals of Hinduism, as of every great religion, are unchangeable, and easily understood. Every Hindu believes in God and His oneness, in rebirth and salvation.[32]

Thus, for Mahatma Gandhi, Vedic authority could not be a dogmatic source of *dharma*, and could never be divorced from actual spirituality, which, for Mahatma Gandhi, was synonymous with morality.[33]

An effort was made to demonstrate above that Mahatma Gandhi can be seen as reversing the order of the sources of *dharma*. The order as found in the Law-books[34] is as follows:

---

32. M.K. Gandhi, *Hindu Dharma*, p. 6; also quoted in T.M.P. Mahadevan, *op. cit.*, p. 7.
33. "I was confirmed in my opinion that religion and morality were synonymous" (M.K. Gandhi, *The Story of My Experiments with Truth*, p. 207).
34. The word *smṛti* is used here not in its broad sense which is inclusive of Itihāsas, Purāṇas and Āgamas, etc., but in a narrower sense. "The works which are expressly called *Smṛti* are law-books, *dharma-śāstras*. Their purpose is to lay down the laws that should guide individuals and communities in their daily conduct and apply the eternal truths of the Veda to the changing conditions of time and clime and thereby preserve the integrity and ensure the progress of Hindu society. From time to time a great law-giver would arise, codify the existing laws, eliminating those which had become obsolete, and see to it that the ways of the Hindus are in a manner consistent with the spirit of the

śruti, smṛti, ācāra and *antaḥkaraṇa.*[35] For Mahatma Gandhi

Veda. Of such law-givers the names of three have become immortal — Manu, Yājñavalkya and Parāśara. And the *Smṛtis* are named after them. Manu is the oldest giver of the law. His work is called *'Mānava-dharmaśāstra,'* the Laws of Man or the Institutes of Manu. Here as well as in the other *Smṛtis* we find instructions to all classes of people regarding their duties in life" (T.M.P. Mahadevan, *op. cit.*, p. 32).

Mahatma Gandhi, though fully aware of the significance of the *Manu-Smṛti* (M.K. Gandhi, *Hindu Dharma*, p. 3, etc.), was not very happy with the text (*ibid.*, p. 239).

35. T.M.P. Mahadevan remarks that: "Much disservice has been done to Hindu society by overlooking the obvious limitations of the *Smṛtis*. It must never be forgotten that whenever there is a conflict between the injunctions of the Veda and the ordinances of the *Smṛti,* the latter must be rejected. And as society advances it may outgrow certain laws which were valid at a particular stage of its development, and it is no use insisting that those out-of-date codes should still be applied. That there are different *Smṛtis* for different times is declared in a Sanskrit verse which reads: 'The laws of Manu are intended for the *Kṛtayuga*; those of Yājñavalkya are for the *Tretāyuga*; those of Śaṅkha and Likhita are for the *Dvāparayuga:* and those of Parāśara are for the *Kaliyuga.'* It is always open to a great reformer or an assembly of wise men to read just old laws to suit the requirements of the age. Another factor which should be remembered is that Manu himself gives an important place for conscience along with the *Veda, Smṛti* and *Ācāra*. We are not to stifle the inner voice in order to conform to external codes. The God within us is the supreme authority in matters of moral action. As the ears of the generality of mankind however are not tuned to this still small voice, there is a need for law-givers and leaders" (*op. cit.*, pp. 32-33).

the order was more like *antaḥkaraṇa, ācāra, smṛti* and *śruti.* That he gave not merely primacy but ultimacy to conscience or morality can be seen from the fact that whenever a question of conflict of morality with any of the other three sources of *dharma* arose, it was always resolved in favour of the latter. Thus when a correspondent asked: "Do you think that sins of touch and sight are of Vedic origin?," he replied:

> Though I cannot speak with authority based on first-hand knowledge, I have full confidence in the purity of the Vedas, and therefore have no hesitation in asserting that the sins of touch and sight have no support in Vedas. I would however add, that no matter what is credited with the Vedic origin if it is repugnant to the moral sense, it must be summarily rejected as contrary to the spirit of the Vedas, and perhaps what is more, as contrary to fundamental ethics.[36]

Mahatma Gandhi similarly gave preference to morality over the authority of the *smṛti*s. Thus he wrote that

> The stories told in the *Purana*s are some of the most dangerous, if we do not know their

---

36. M.K. Gandhi, *Hindu Dharma,* p. 281. Mahatma Gandhi did not regard himself as a Vedic scholar and therefore could not "speak with authority based on firsthand knowledge." Those who can have pointed out that the Vedic origin of the "sins of touch and sight" is very doubtful, to say the least (see R.C. Majumdar, ed., *The Vedic Age* [London: George Allen & Unwin Ltd., 1957], pp. 384, 388).

> bearing on the present conditions.[37]

And one of his favourite books, the *Rāmacaritamānasa* of Tulsīdās he wrote:

> Another canon of interpretation is to scan not the letter but to examine the spirit. Tulsidas' *Ramayana* is a notable book because it is informed with the spirit of purity, pity and piety. There is a verse in it which brackets drums, Shudras, fools and women together as fit to be beaten. A man who cites that verse to beat his wife is doomed to perdition. Rama did not only not beat his wife, but never even sought to displease her. Tulsidas simply inserted in his poem a proverb current in his days, little dreaming that there would be brutes justifying beating their wives on the authority of the verse. But assuming that Tulsidas himself followed a custom which was prevalent in his days and beat his wife, what then? The beating was still wrong. But the *Ramayana* was not written to justify beating of wives by their husbands. It was written to depict Rama, the perfect man, and Sita the ideal wife, and Bharata the ideal of a devoted brother. Any justification incidentally met with therein of vicious customs would therefore be rejected. Tulsidas did not write his priceless epic to teach geography, and any wrong geography that we happen to come across in *Ramayana* should be summarily rejected.[38]

---

37. M.K. Gandhi, *Hindu Dharma*, p. 21.

38. *Ibid.*, p. 136.

But Tulsīdās's *Rāmāyaṇa* can be classed as a *smṛti* only in an extended sense.[39] In the case of the *Gītā*, Mahatma Gandhi said that ever since he first read them in Edwin Arnold's translation,[40]

> The last nineteen verses of the second chapter have since been inscribed on the tablet of my

---

39. See T.M.P. Mahadevan, *op. cit.*, p. 39.

40. "Towards the end of my second year in England I came across two Theosophists, brothers, and both unmarried. They talked to me about the *Gita*. They were reading Sir Edwin Arnold's translation, *The Song Celestial*, and they invited me to read the original with them. I felt ashamed, as I had read the divine poem neither in Sanskrit nor in Gujarati. I was constrained to tell them that I had not read the *Gita*, but that I would gladly read it with them, and that though my knowledge of Sanskrit was meager, still I hoped to be able to understand the original to the extent of telling where the translation failed to bring out the meaning. I began reading the *Gita* with them. The verses in the second chapter

    If one
    Ponders on objects of the sense, there springs
    Attraction; from attraction grows desire,
    Desire flames to fierce passion, passion breeds
    Recklessness; then the mercy — all betrayed —
    Lets noble purpose go, and sap the mind,
    Till purpose, mind, and man are all undone.

    made a deep impression on my mind, and they still ring in my ears. The book struck me as one of priceless worth. The impression has ever since been growing on me with the result that I regard it today as the book *par excellence* for the knowledge of Truth. It has afforded me invaluable help in

> heart. They contain for me all knowledge. The truths they teach are "eternal verities." There is reasoning in them but they represent realized knowledge.[41]

Then Mahatma Gandhi goes on to remark:

> I have since read many translations and many commentaries, have argued and reasoned to my heart's content but the impression that the first reading gave me has never been effaced. Those verses are the key to the interpretation of the *Gita*. I would even advise rejection of the verses that may seem to be in conflict with them. But a humble student need reject nothing. He will simply say: "It is the limitation of my own intellect that I cannot resolve this inconsistency. I might be able to do so in the time to come." That is how he will plead with himself and with others.[42]

Mahatma Gandhi is even prepared to reject verses of the *Gītā* although he moderates his stand after saying so. The crux of the matter is that the first two sources of *dharma* represent scriptural authority as the basis of *dharma*, and Mahatma Gandhi was never prepared to concede

---

my moments of gloom. I have read almost all the English translations of it, and I regard Sir Edwin Arnold's as the best. He has been faithful to the text, and yet it does not read like a translation" (M.K. Gandhi, *The Story of My Experiments with Truth*, p. 90).

41. M.K. Gandhi, *Hindu Dharma*, p. 135.
42. *Ibid.*

supremacy to scriptural authority when it conflicted with morality. This is brought out pointedly in his discussions on the scriptural basis of untouchability. He writes:

> My message is exceedingly simple. It is no new truth that has dawned upon me today. I have to the best of my ability striven to live up to it for the past fifty years. And the more I have succeeded in living up to it, the greater has been my inward joy. Nor is it for the first time that I am delivering this message to India. But because of some incidents in the recent past, it comes to the people as a new thing. My message is simply this that *savarna* Hindus, who have been considering themselves superior to those whom they have called untouchables, unapproachables, invisibles, or *avarna* Hindus, should realise that this arrogation of superiority has no sanction whatsoever in the *shastras*. *If I had discovered that those scriptures which are known as the Vedas, the Upanishads, the Bhagavadgita, the Smritis, etc., clearly showed that they claimed divine authority for untouchability as I have described to you, then nothing on this earth would hold me to Hinduism.* I should throw it overboard as I should throw overboard a rotten apple. My reason is offended and my heart is wounded at the very thought that God Himself who has created both *savarna* Hindus and *avarna* Hindus, should impose this bar sinister between His children. The very thought that the *rishis*, who gave the *Vedas* and the *Upanishads* and who in every *mantra* that they pronounced taught the unity of God,

> could ever conceive of any such thing as untouchability as it is practised today in Hinduism must be repugnant to every intelligent person. They cloud the reason, befog the intellect and harden the heart. And so you find learned men defending this untouchability.[43]

As a matter of fact Mahatma Gandhi took a dynamic view of the scriptures. In theological jargon he could be said to be a believer in continuous revelation.[44] At another level he can be said to be a believer in the maxim that "time makes ancient good uncouth" and that laws and usages must change with the times.[45] Recognition of this fact is implicit in Hindu thought[46] and has even been recognized explicitly by some Hindu thinkers in the past[47] but Mahatma Gandhi used these ideas in conjunction with the doctrine that moral considerations outweigh all other sources of Law and thus could offer an explicitly dynamic hermeneutics:

---

43. *Ibid.*, p. 307, emphasis added.
44. See K. Satchidananda Murty, *op. cit.*, Part II, Chapter III, IV, V.
45. See M.K. Gandhi, *Hindu Dharma*, pp. 19-21.
46. See T.M.P. Mahadevan, *op. cit.*, pp. 32-33.
47. See P.V. Kane, *History of Dharmaśāstra*, vol. V (Part II) (Poona: Bhandarkar Oriental Research Institute, 1962), pp. 1267-72, 1471, etc. G.S. Ghurye, however, seems to think that this was not commonly acknowledged: "Mādhava makes a frank and *rare* admission that the practices and regulations about the four castes have been changing from age to age" (*Caste and Race in India* [Bombay: Popular Prakashan, 1969], p. 106, emphasis added).

Hinduism is a living organism liable to growth and decay, and subject to the laws of Nature. One and indivisible at the root it has grown into a vast tree with innumerable branches. The changes in the seasons affect it. It has its autumn and summer, its winter and spring. The rains nourish and fructify it too. It is and is not based on scriptures. It does not derive its authority from one book. The *Gita* is universally accepted, but even then it only shows the way. It has hardly any effect on custom. Hinduism is like the Ganga pure and unsullied at its source, but taking in its course the impurities in the way. Even like the Ganga it is beneficent in its total effect. It takes a provincial form in every province, but the inner substance is retained everywhere. Custom is not religion. Custom may change, but religion will remain unaltered.

Purity of Hinduism depends on the self-restraint of its votaries. Whenever their religion has been in danger, the Hindus have undergone rigorous penance, searched the causes of danger and devised means for combating them. The *shastra*s are ever growing. The *Veda*s, the *Upanishad*s, the *Smriti*s, the *Purana*s, and the *Itihasa*s did not arise at one and the same time. Each grew out of the necessities of particular periods, and therefore they seem to conflict with one another. These books do not enunciate anew the eternal truths but show how these were practised at the time to which the books belong. A practice which was good enough in a particular period would, if blindly repeated in another, land people into the "slough of despond." Because the practice of animal-sacrifice obtained at one time shall we revive it today? Because at one time we used to eat beef, shall we also do so now? Because at one time we used to chop off the hands and feet of thieves, shall we revive that barbarity today? Shall we revive polyandry? Shall we revive child-marriage? Because we discarded a section of humanity one day, shall we brand their descendants today as outcastes?[48]

48. M.K. Gandhi, *Hindu Dharma*, p. 19. Mahatma Gandhi however, rejected scriptural authority when it conflicted with morality but when it upheld morality he used it to support his own position. Thus he could say that "How in the face of the fact that no scriptural text mentions a fifth *varna*, and in the face of the express injunction of the *Gita* to regard a *brahmana* and a *bhangi* as equals we persist in maintaining this deep blot on Hinduism (i.e. untouchability). I cannot understand" (*ibid.*, p. 173). He could also on occasion argue that: "I give the same credit to those who call themselves *Sanatanists* for honesty of purpose that I would claim for myself, but both must have an equal right to give expression to their views and mould public opinion. After all, *Sanatana Dharma* is not the prerogative of one set of people. I claim myself to be a representative of *Sanatana Dharma* in every sense of the term that they claim. I base my vehement opposition to untouchability upon the same *shastra*s by which they swear, and I should stand by my interpretation of the *shastra*s even though I were the solitary one amongst the millions of Hindus; because the

Not only was thus morality to supersede scriptural authority — whether Vedic or non-Vedic as a source of *dharma*, it was also superior to *ācāra*. Mahatma Gandhi remarked consistently with this position:

> But I must not be misunderstood. I do not hold that everything ancient is good because it is ancient. I do not advocate surrender of God-given reasoning faculty in the face of ancient tradition. Any tradition, however ancient, if inconsistent with morality, is fit to be banished from the land. Untouchability may be considered to be an ancient tradition, the institution of child-widowhood and child-marriage may be considered to be ancient tradition, and even so many an ancient horrible belief and superstitious practice. I would sweep them out of existence if I had the power.[49]

---

same *shastras* tell me that I may not resist the inner call of my fundamental being. Thank God, however, that I do not stand alone in the interpretation that I have been placing before you. On the contrary, there are learned *shastris* who have just as much right to interpret the *shastras* as those who call themselves the exponents of *Sanatana Dharma*. And they give precisely the same interpretation that I have placed before tens of thousands of men and women. And it is my settled conviction, based upon an unbroken experience extending over a period of nearly fifty years, that untouchability as we practice it today has absolutely no warrant whatsoever in Hindu *shastras*" (*ibid.*, p. 295).

49. M.K. Gandhi, *Hindu Dharma*, pp. 257-58.

It is clear, then, that Mahatma Gandhi could be seen as having reversed the priorities among the acknowledged sources of *dharma* in the Hindu religious tradition.[50] In any

50. R.C. Zaehner institutes an interesting comparison between Yudhiṣṭhira and Mahatma Gandhi. He writes that Mahatma Gandhi "described himself as a *sanatani* Hindu, one who follows the *sanatana dharma,* the 'eternal law' once embodied in the *dharma-raja,* Yudhishthira. And Gandhi's dilemma was the same as Yudhishthira's: what and where *was* the *sanatana dharma* he claimed to follow? Was it in his heart or was it in the Brahmans proclaim?

    The Christian missionaries had many faults — 'I miss receptiveness, humility, willingness on your part to identify yourselves with the masses of India,' he had told them in Calcutta — but they had pointed accusing fingers at abuses that shocked the conscience of the world — and the greatest of these was untouchability. According to the brahmans, untouchability was part and parcel of the *sanatana dharma,* and the *Laws of Manu* seemed to bear them out. From his childhood, however, Gandhi had found untouchability absurd; in his later life he was to find it revolting and he refused to cooperate with anyone who failed to denounce it. In what, then, did his 'orthodoxy' consist?

    It will be remembered that Yudhishthira was tortured by the same agonizing doubts. Was it the *dharma* preached by the brahmans that was the 'eternal' *dharma,* or was it the *dharma* that was the well-spring of his being, the *dharma* by virtue of which he was the 'King of *dharma*' — 'King of Righteousness' because the conscience of a truthful man cannot lead astray? He hesitated because God himself had driven him into violence and war, and had made him lie, but he nevertheless *knew* that his conscience transcended

case, he altered them, giving the pride of place to morality

---

the 'righteousness' of the Brahmans and of Krishna himself. Yudhishthira's dilemma was more agonizing, more searching than Gandhi's was ever to be. *His* conscience was the first to protest against a violent and unjust society; there had been no reformers before him. Gandhi was luckier, for he had been preceded by the Brahmo Samaj which had openly denounced caste, untouchability, and a host of other questionable institutions, and had challenged the infallible authority of the Vedas themselves; he had before his eyes too the Arya Samaj of Dayananda whose interpretation of the Veda was so utterly at variance with that of the orthodox that plainly one could do with the sacred texts almost anything one liked. So it seemed only natural that he could say of the scriptures, 'My belief in the Hindu Scriptures does not require me to accept every word and every verse as divinely inspired. Nor do I claim to have any first-hand knowledge of these wonderful books. But I do claim to know and feel the truths of the essential teachings of the Scriptures. I decline to be bound by any interpretation, however learned it may be, if it is repugnant to reason and moral sense.' The outraged conscience of Yudhishthira speaks through the lips of Mahatma Gandhi. And Gandhi's God too is the God of Yudhishthira, not the God of *bhakti* or of the philosophers. 'To me God is Truth and Love; God is *ethics and morality'* God is fearlessness; God is the source of Light and Life, and yet he is above and beyond all these. *God is conscience.* God is, in fact, what Gandhi in his heart feels him to be: he is not the God of the law-books or even of the Vedas, should these prove to conflict with the light within them" (*op. cit.*, pp. 170-72).

Elsewhere he makes a more straightforward comparison: "Yudhishthira was 'steadfast, self-restrained, chaste,

or conscience.[51]

---

patient, ever devoted to *dharma*, high-mettled; he honoured and gave hospitality to guests, relatives, servants, and all who had resort to him; truthful, generous, ascetic, brave, he was at peace with himself, wise, and imperturbable; himself the soul of *dharma*, he never committed an injustice out of desire or yielding to impetuosity, out of fear, or to promote his own interests.' The same was true of Mahatma Gandhi, the Yudhishthira of his age" (*ibid.*, p. 178, but also see p. 179).

In view of Mahatma Gandhi's views about the mutability of human institutions it is interesting to note "Yudhisthira's comment in the *Mahabharata* that institutions are man-made, and they are but imperfect manifestations, according to time and place, of eternal values which are hard for man to know" (Pratima Bowes, *The Hindu Religious Tradition* [London: Routledge and Kegan Paul, 1979], p. 312). It may be added, however, on the evidence of the *Mahābhārata* that R.C. Zaehner's emphasis on the role of conscience in Yudhiṣṭhira may involve some measure of overstatement as at least in one context it is said that *mahājano yena gataḥ sa panthāḥ* (the course to be followed in case of doubts about *dharma* is the one adopted by great men), which seems to accord a strong role to *ācāra* in the sense of exemplary conduct as a source of *dharma*.

51. For more on how Mahatma Gandhi evolved his personal and eclectic faith see J.T.F. Jordens, *Gandhi's Religion: A Homespun Shawl* (London: The MacMillan Company, 1998).

2

Mahatma Gandhi and Untouchability

Mahatma Gandhi seems to have been profoundly influenced by his aversion to untouchability in his attitude to the sources of *dharma*. "I may be bold to say," he said, "that there is no warrant whatsoever in Hinduism for untouchability as it is practiced today."[1] But before one can appreciate the role of Mahatma Gandhi's position on untouchability in affecting his priorities among the sources of *dharma*, the full extent of his aversion to it needs to be realized. It is helpful here to realize how early his position on the question crystallized.[2] He writes:

---

1. M.K. Gandhi, *Hindu Dharma*, p. 31.
2. "In his youth, Gandhi played with an untouchable boy. Putlibai forbade it. Though he loved her he disobeyed her, his first rebellion against authority. 'I used to laugh at my dear mother,' he wrote to Charles Freer Andrews, 'for making us bathe when we brothers touched any pariah.' In South Africa, too, he associated with untouchables. In May, 1918, in Bombay, he went to a meeting called to improve the lot of untouchables. When he got up to deliver his address, he said, 'Is there an untouchable here?' No hand was raised. Gandhi refused to speak. Now there came to Gandhi's ashram near Ahmedabad an untouchable family and asked

> My views on untouchability are not the product of my Western education. I had formed them long before I went to England, and long before I studied the scriptures, and in an atmosphere which was by no means favourable to those views. For I was born in an orthodox Vaishnava family and yet ever since I reached the year of discretion I have firmly held my uncompromising views in the matter, which later comparative study of Hinduism and experience have only confirmed.[3]

Robert Payne provided the following interesting details:

> It was a time when he was beginning to think seriously about morality and codes of conduct. He was twelve, in his second year at the high school, when he began to question the accepted codes of the Indian caste system. A scavenger called Uka, who belonged to the lowest caste, was employed in the house to clean out the latrines. If anyone of a superior caste accidentally touched the scavenger, then he must at once purify himself by performing his ablutions. Mohandas had a great fondness for Uka and could see no reason why he should be regarded as an inferior. Very respectfully he suggested to his parents that they were

---

to become permanent members. He admitted them." (Louis Fischer, *op. cit.*, p. 143). It is important to realize that Mahatma Gandhi did not share the maternal prejudice notwithstanding his devotion to his parents, of which his autobiography provides ample evidence.

3. M.K. Gandhi, *Hindu Dharma*, p. 173.

> wrong to regard the scavenger in this way; an accidental touch could not be a sin and Uka was a man like other men. His mother reminded him that it was not necessary to perform one's ablutions after touching a scavenger; instead, one could touch a Muslim, thus transferring the pollution to someone who was free of the taboos of the Hindu religion.[4]

Not only is Mahatma Gandhi's position on the issue remarkable for its precocity, it is also remarkable for its intensity. Mahatma Gandhi's bitterest marital conflict with Kasturba occurred over this issue. The incident finds a prominent place in his *Autobiography* and is recorded as follows:

> A variety of incidents in my life have conspired to bring me in close contact with people of many creeds and many com-munities, and my experience with all of them warrants the statement that I have known no distinction between relatives and strangers, countrymen and foreigners, white and coloured, Hindus and Indians of other faiths, whether Musalmans, Parsis, Christians or Jews. I may say that my heart has been incapable of making any such distinctions. I cannot claim this as a special virtue, as it is in my very nature, rather than a result of any effort on my part, whereas in the case of *ahimsa* (non-violence), *brahmacharya* (celibacy), *aparigraha* (non-

4. Robert Payne, *The Life and Death of Mahatma Gandhi* (New York: E.P. Dutton & Co., 1969), p. 34.

possession) and other cardinal virtues, I am fully conscious of a continuous striving for their cultivation.

When I was practising in Durban, my office clerks often stayed with me, and there were among them Hindus and Christians, or to describe them by their provinces, Gujaratis and Tamilians. I do not recollect having ever regarded them as anything but my kith and kin. I treated them as members of my family, and had unpleasantness with my wife if ever she stood in the way of my treating them as such. One of the clerks was a Christian, born of Panchama parents.

The house was built after the Western model and the rooms rightly had no outlets for dirty water. Each room had therefore chamber-pots. Rather than have these cleaned by a servant or a sweeper, my wife or I attended to them. The clerks who made themselves completely at home would naturally clean their own pots, but the Christian clerk was a newcomer, and it was our duty to attend to his bedroom. My wife managed the pots of the others, but to clean those used by one who had been a Panchama seemed to her to be the limit, and we fell out. She could not bear the pots being cleaned by me, neither did she like doing it herself. Even today I can recall the picture of her chiding me, her eyes red with anger, and pearl drops streaming down her cheeks, as she descended the ladder, pot in hand. But I was a cruelly kind husband. I regarded myself as her teacher, and so harassed her out of my blind love for her.

I was far from being satisfied by her merely carrying the pot. I would have her do it cheerfully. So I said, raising my voice: 'I will not stand this nonsense in my house.'

The words pieced her like an arrow.

She shouted back: 'Keep your house to yourself and let me go.' I forgot myself, and the spring of compassion dried up in me. I caught her by the hand, dragged the helpless woman to the gate, which was just opposite the ladder, and proceeded to open it with the intention of pushing her out. The tears were running down her cheeks in torrents, and she cried: 'Have you no sense of shame? Must you so far forget yourself? Where am I to go? I have no parents or relatives here to harbour me. Being your wife, you think I must put up with your cuffs and kicks? For Heaven's sake behave yourself, and shut the gate. Let us not be found making scenes like this!'

I put on a brave face, but was really ashamed and shut the gate. If my wife could not leave me, neither could I leave her. We have had numerous bickerings, but the end has always been peace between us. The wife, with her matchless powers of endurance, has always been the victor.

> Today I am in a position to narrate the incident with some detachment, as it belongs to a period out of which I have fortunately emerged. I am no longer a blind, infatuated husband. I am no more my wife's teacher. Kasturba can, if she will, be as unpleasant to me today, as I used to be to her before. We are tried friends, the one no longer regarding the other as the object of lust. She has been a faithful nurse throughout my illnesses, serving without any thought of reward.[5]

From the point of view of this chapter, of course, it is not the matrimonial but the moral aspect of the situation which is central. The difference between them arose over the fact that Kasturba was being pressured by Mahatma Gandhi to clean the chamber-pot of "a Christian, born of *pancama* parents," i.e., an untouchable. Hence it was really Mahatma Gandhi's personal conviction that untouchability was immoral which seems to account for his giving conscience top priority as a source of *dharma*. The following passage in the *Young India* of 27-4-1921 brings out the interplay of the four sources in this context clearly:

> I have always claimed to be a *Sanatani* Hindu. It is not that I am quite innocent of the scriptures. I am not a profound scholar of Sanskrit. I have read the Vedas and the Upanishads only in translation. Naturally therefore mine is not a scholarly study of them. My knowledge of them is in no way profound,

5. M.K. Gandhi, *The Story of My Experiments with Truth*, pp. 338-41.

but I have studied them as I should do as a Hindu and I claim to have grasped their true spirit. By the time I had reached the age of 21, I had studied other religions also.

There was a time when I was wavering between Hinduism and Christianity. When I recovered my balance of mind, I felt that to me salvation was possible only through the Hindu religion and my faith in Hinduism grew deeper and more enlightened.

But even then I believed that untouchability was no part of Hinduism; and that, if it was, such Hinduism was not for me.

True, Hinduism does not regard untouchability as a sin. I do not want to enter into any controversy regarding the interpretation of the *shastras*. It might be difficult for me to establish my point by quoting authorities from the *Bhagavata* or the *Manusmrti*. But I claim to have understood the spirit of Hinduism. Hinduism has sinned in giving sanction to untouchability. It has degraded us, made us the pariahs of the Empire. Even the Mussulmans caught the sinful contagion from us, and in South Africa, in East Africa and in Canada the Mussulmans no less than the Hindus came to be regarded as pariahs. All this evil has resulted from the sin of untouchability.[6]

---

6. Quoted in M.K. Gandhi, *Hindu Dharma*, p. 279.

Mahatma Gandhi identifies the "spirit of Hinduism" as he feels it to be as the basis of his position.[7] With regard to the Smṛtis he admits that "it might be difficult for me to establish my point by quoting authorities," which implies that he was at least familiar with them.[8] His familiarity with the Vedas is admitted to be less.[9] But he did appeal to example or *ācāra* as when he cited the instance of Rāma eating berries at the hands of the "scheduled caste" Śabarī.

Much more difficult was Mahatma Gandhi's attempt to taste these berries himself. The first taste was bitter. In September 1916 the first untouchable couple entered the *āśrama* at Sabarmati.

---

7. "The simplest explanation of Gandhi's attitude toward untouchability is that he just could not stand it. In fact, he loathed this 'inhuman boycott of human beings' so much that he said 'if it was proved to me that it is an essential part of Hinduism I for one would declare myself an open rebel against Hinduism itself.' No man who cared more for popularity than principle would have made a public statement in a country overwhelmingly and conservatively Hindu. But he made it as a Hindu in an effort, he said, to purify his religion. He regarded untouchability as an 'excrescence,' a perversion of Hinduism" (Louis Fischer, *op. cit.*, p. 146).

8. This is confirmed by a perusal of his autobiography; see M.K. Gandhi, *The Story of My Experiments with Truth*, pp. 47-50.

9. With the Vedic corpus, however, he seems to have been drawn especially to the opening verse of the *Īśa Upaniṣad*, see M.K. Gandhi, *Hindu Dharma*, p. 304; T.M.P. Mahadevan, *op. cit.*, pp. 26-27.

> A Bombay teacher called Dudabbhai, his wife Danibehn and baby daughter Lakshmi, belonging to the untouchable class of *Dheds* were invited into the ashram. At once there was uproar. Kasturba threatened to leave the Ashram. Gandhi answered that it would be extremely painful to him if she left, but he would not prevent her. She must observe the rules or leave. So the tempest subsided.[10]

This private tempest was nothing compared to the public tempest which followed. The textile magnates who were supporting the *āśrama* began to withdraw their support.

> One by one they withdrew their support, until the time came when the ashram had no money at all. Gandhi was not in the least dismayed. God in His infinite goodness would provide, and if not, then they could always go and live in the untouchable quarter of Ahmedabad. One day an automobile drove up to the ashram and paused long enough for someone to pass an envelope into Gandhi's hands. When the mysterious visitor left, Gandhi opened the envelope to discover thirteen thousand rupees in banknotes. Such miracles were not uncommon and in time Gandhi came to depend on them.[11]

Mahatma Gandhi has fallen back on conscience as the ultimate source of *dharma* and somehow it had worked.

---

10. Robert Payne, *op. cit.*, pp. 293-94.
11. *Ibid.*

3

Mahatma Gandhi and the Caste System

The recognition of the role that Mahatma Gandhi's attitude towards untouchability played in determining his priorities among the sources of *dharma* recognized in Hinduism provides a useful transition to the next set of priorities within the Hindu religious tradition which Mahatma Gandhi at least upset or even reversed — those related to the Caste System. It is well-known that:

> Relations between classes and social groups in later Hinduism were governed by rules of endogamy (marriage was only legitimate within the group), commensality (food was only to be received from and eaten in the presence of the members of the same or a higher group), and craft-exclusiveness (each man was to live by the trade and profession of his own group, and not take up that of another).[1]

This arrangement is loosely referred to as the Caste System. But the word must be used with caution for as has been pointed out that:

---

1. A.L. Basham, *The Wonder that was India* (New York: Taplinger Publishing Company, 1967), pp. 148-49.

When the Portuguese came to India in the 16th century they found the Hindu community divided into many separate groups, which they called *castas*, meaning tribes, clans or families. The name stuck, and became the usual word for the Hindu social group. In attempting to account for the remarkable proliferation of castes in the 18th and 19th century India, authorities credulously accepted the traditional view that by a process of intermarriage and subdivision the 3000 or more castes of modern India had evolved from the four primitive classes, and the term "caste" was applied indiscriminately to both *varṇa* or class, and *jāti* or caste proper. This is a false terminology; castes rise and fall in the social scale, and old castes die out and new ones are formed, but the four great classes are stable. They are never more or less than four, and for over 2000 years their order of precedence has not altered. All ancient Indian sources make a sharp distinction between the two terms; *varṇa* is much referred to, but *jāti* very little, and when it does appear in literature it does not always imply the comparatively rigid and exclusive social group of later times. If caste is defined as a system of groups within the same class which are normally endogamous, commensal and craft-exclusive, we have no real evidence of its existence until comparatively late times.[2]

---

2. A.L. Basham, *The Wonder that was India* (New York: Taplinger Publishing Company, 1967), p. 149. P.V. Kane notes, however, that although "Varna and jati are sometimes

Mahatma Gandhi lived in these "comparatively late times" in which, on the Hindu social scene, *jāti* and *varṇa* had been confounded, with a heavy admixture of the former at the expense of the latter.[3] It is this phenomenon which is usually described by the word caste.[4] In other words, as between *jāti* and *varṇa,* Hindu priority in practice at times

---

clearly distinguished . . . very often they are confounded" in Smṛti literature (*op. cit.*, vol. II, Part I, p. 55). But also see Percival Spear, ed., *The Oxford History of India* (Oxford: Clarendon Press, 1958) pp. 63-64.

3. It has been observed that "To the present day the life of the lower orders is much more affected by caste than by varna — it is not being a vaiśya or a śūdra, but being an *ahīr*, a *kāyasth*, or a *sonār* which matters — and corporate feeling is centered around the caste group, whether based on region, profession or religion" (*ibid.*, p. 150). It should be noted that in this passage the word caste has been used in the sense of *jāti.*

4. "*Definition of a caste.* A caste may be defined as a group of families internally united by peculiar rules for the observance of ceremonial purity, especially in the matters of diet and marriage. The same rules serve to fence it off from all the other groups, each of which has its own set of rules. Admission to an established caste in long settled territory can be obtained nowadays by birth only, and transitions from one caste to another, which used to be feasible in ancient times, are no longer possible, except in frontier regions like Manipur. The families composing a caste may or may not have traditions of descent from a common ancestor, and, as a matter of fact, may or may not belong to one stock. Race, that is to say, descent by blood, has little concern with caste, in northern India, at all events, whatever may be the case in the south. The individual

lay in favour of *jāti.* Mahatma Gandhi reversed this priority

members of a caste may or may not be restricted to any particular occupation or occupations. The members may believe or disbelieve any creed or doctrine, religious or philosophical, without affecting their caste position. That can be forfeited only by breach of the caste regulations concerning the *dharma*, or practical duty of members belonging to the group. Each caste has its own *dharma*, in addition to the common rules of morality as accepted by Hindus generally, and considered to be the *dharma* of mankind. The general Hindu *dharma* exacts among other things reverence to Brahmans, respect for the sanctity of animal life in varying degrees, and especially veneration for horned cattle, pre-eminently the cow. Every caste man is expected to observe accurately the rules of his own group, and to refrain from doing violence to the feelings of other groups concerning their rules. The essential duty of the member of a caste is to follow the custom of his group, more particularly in relation to diet or marriage. Violation of the rules on these subjects, if detected, usually involves unpleasant and costly social expiation and may result in expulsion from the caste, which means social ruin and grave inconvenience.

The Hindus have not any name for the caste institution, which seems to them part of the order of nature. It is almost impossible for a Hindu to regard himself otherwise than as a member of some particular caste, or species of Hindu mankind. Everyone else who disregards Hindu *dharma* is an 'outer barbarian' (*mlechchha*) no matter how exalted his worldly rank or how vast his wealth may be. The proper Sanskrit and vernacular term for 'a caste' is *jāti* (*jāt*), 'species,' although as noted above, the members of a *jāti* are not necessarily descended from a common ancestor. Indeed, as a matter of fact, they are rarely, if ever, so descended. Their

in his own scheme of things by insisting that he stood for

---

special caste rules make their community in effect a distinct species, whoever their ancestors may have been.

The fiction of four original castes. The common notion that there were four original castes, Brahman, Kshatriya, or Rājanya, Vaiśya, and Śūdra, is false. The ancient Hindu writers classified mankind under four *varnas* or 'orders,' with reference to their occupations, namely: (1) the learned, literature, and priestly order, or Brahmans; (2) the fighting and governing classes, who are grouped together as Rājanyas or Kshatriyas, irrespective of race, meaning by that term ancestry; (3) the trading and agricultural people, or Vaiśyas; and (4) common, humble fold, day labourers, and so forth, whose business it was to serve their betters. Every family and caste (*jāti*) observing Hindu *dharma* necessarily fell under one or other of those four heads. Various half-wild tribes, and also communities like sweepers, whose occupations are obviously unclean, were regarded as standing outside the four orders or *varṇas*. Such unclean communities have usually imitated the Hindu caste organisation and developed an elaborate system of castes of their own, which may be described by the paradoxical term 'out-caste castes.'

Nobody can understand the caste system until he has freed himself from the mistaken notion based on the current interpretation of the so-called *Institutes of Manu,* that there were 'four original castes.' No four original castes ever existed at any time or place, and at the present moment the terms Kshatriya, Vaiśya, and Śūdra have no exact meaning as a classification of existing castes. In northern India the names Vaiśya and Śūdra are not used except in books or disputes about questions of caste precedence. In the south all Hindus who are not Brahmans fall under the *varṇa* and not *jāti*.[5] Thus in a speech delivered at Trivandrum on 9-10-1927 he declared:

> As years go by, the conviction is daily growing upon me that *varna* is the law of man's being and therefore as necessary for Christianity and Islam, as it has been necessary for Hinduism and as it has been its saving. I refuse, therefore, to believe that *varnashrama* has been the curse of Hinduism, as it is the fashion nowadays in the South on the part of some Hindus to say. But that does not mean that you and I may tolerate for one moment or be gentle towards the hideous travesty of *varnashrama* that we see about us today. There is nothing in common

---

denomination of Śūdra, while the designations Kshatriya and Vaiśya are practically unknown." Percival Spear, *op. cit.*, pp. 61-62.

5. "Varna has nothing to do with caste. Down with the monster of caste that masquerades in the guise of *varna*. It is this travesty of *varna* that has degraded Hinduism and India" (M.K. Gandhi, *Hindu Dharma*, p. 376). The word caste seems to have been clearly used in the sense of *jāti* here: "But restrictions on marital or social relations have nothing to do with *Varna Dharma,* which is a different thing altogether. I can conceive blameless marital relations between different *varnas*, and people of different *varnas* seated together to eat food permissible to all. There is evidence enough to show that in ancient times there were no watertight compartments between *varnas*, so far as marital and social relations went, and I have no doubt that, in making *varna* a mere matter of restrictions about food and drink and marriage, we have done Hinduism grave harm" (*ibid.*, p. 338).

> between *varnashrama* and caste. Caste, if you will, is undoubtedly a drag upon Hindu progress, and untouchability is, as I have already called it or described it, an excrescence upon *varnashrama.* It is a weedy growth fit only to be weeded out, as we weed out the weeds that we see growing in wheat fields or rice fields. In this conception of *varna,* there is absolutely no idea of superiority and inferiority. If I again interpret the Hindu spirit rightly all life is absolutely equal and one. It is therefore an arrogant assumption on the part of the *brahmana* when he says, 'I am superior to the other three varnas.' That is not what the *brahmanas* of old said.[6]

After thus opting for *varṇa* against *jāti,* Mahatma Gandhi had to face the next question: on what is *varṇa* based? The Hindu social reality has been that *varṇa* has been based on *janma* or birth much more than on *karma* or action. Now Mahatma Gandhi did not deny that birth was not important. For him "the law of *varṇa* is nothing if not by birth,"[7] but he shifted the balance in favour of *karma.* That is to say, if actions of a member of the *varṇa* were not consistent with his birth into that *varṇa,* the person lost his *varṇa* status. Mahatma Gandhi remarked:

> *Varna* is determined by birth, but can be retained only by observing its obligations. One born of *brahmana* parents will be called a *brahmana,* but if his life fails to reveal the

---

6. M.K. Gandhi, *Hindu Dharma,* p. 324.

7. *Ibid.,* p. 330.

> attributes of a *brahmana* when he comes of age, he cannot be called a *brahmana*. He will have fallen from *brahmanahood*. On the other hand, one who is born not a *brahmana* but reveals in his conduct the attributes of a *brahmana* will be regarded as a *brahmana*, though he will himself disclaim the label.[8]

Even with the word *varṇa* being used in the ideal sense, the Hindu theory of *varṇa* envisages four *varṇas*.[9] This classification Mahatma Gandhi accepted and wrote:

> That brings us to a consideration of the law of *varna*. *Varna* is intimately, if not indissolubly, connected with birth, and the observance of the law of *varna* means the following on the part of all of the hereditary and traditional calling of our forefathers in a spirit of duty. Those who fulfil the law of their *varna* can be counted on one's fingers' ends. This performance of one's hereditary function is done as a matter of duty, though it naturally carries with it the earning of one's livelihood. Thus, the function of a *brahmana* is to study and to teach the science of *Brahman* (or spiritual truth). He performs the function, as he cannot do otherwise, as it is the law of his being. That secures him in his livelihood, but he will take it as a gift from God. A *kshatriya* will perform the function of protecting the people in the

8. M.K. Gandhi, *Hindu Dharma*, p. 337.
9. Kenneth W. Morgan, ed., *The Religion of the Hindus* (New York: The Ronald Press Company, 1953), p. 6.

> same spirit, accepting his livelihood whatever the people can afford to give him. A *vaishya* will pursue wealth-producing occupations for the welfare of the community, keeping for himself enough for his own maintenance and rendering the balance to the community in one shape or other. A *shudra* will perform physical labour in the same spirit of service.[10]

This classification of the four orders, however, is often seen in the Hindu religious tradition as implying a gradation.[11]

---

10. M.K. Gandhi, *Hindu Dharma,* p. 337.
11. This was challenged by Mahatma Gandhi who argued that the comparison of the four *varṇa*s to the four limbs of the body did not imply a hierarchy. Thus he wrote:

    > The four *varna*s have been compared in the *Veda*s to the four members of the body, and no simile could be happier. If they are members of one body, how can one be superior or inferior to another? If the members of the body had the power of expression and each of them were to say that it was higher and better than the rest, the body would go to pieces. Even so, our body politic, the body of humanity, would go to pieces, if it were to perpetuate the canker of superiority or inferiority. It is this canker that is at the root of the various ills of our time, especially class-wars and civil strife. It should not be difficult for even the meanest understanding to see that these wars and strifes could not be ended except for the observance of the law of *varna*. For it ordains that every one shall fulfil the law of one's being by doing in a spirit of duty and service that to which one is born (*ibid.,* p. 339).

And sometimes the untouchables actually fell outside this gradation and were called *pañcama*s or the fifth. Thus one could enumerate the traditional ordering as follows: (1) brāhmaṇa; (2) kṣatriya; (3) vaiśya; (4) śūdra; (5) *pañcama*. Normally brāhmaṇas are supposed to comprise

---

He further argued that as no one was following the *varṇa* system anyway all Hindus really belonged to the same *varṇa*.

> If I had the power, I would declare that we are all Hindus, all of the same *varna*. *As I have made it clear over and over again there is no real varna today.* When we have come to our own, when we have cleansed ourselves, we may have the four *varnas* according to the way in which we can express the best in us. But *varna* will then invest no one with a superior status or right, it will invest one with higher responsibility and duties. Those who will impart knowledge in a spirit of service will be called *brahmanas*. They will assume no superior airs but will be true servants of society. When inequality of status or rights is ended, every one of us will be equal. I do not know, however, when we shall be able to revive true *Varna Dharma*. Its real revival would mean true democracy (*ibid.*, emphasis added).

This *varṇa* to which all Hindus belonged now was the śūdra *varṇa* according to him. At one point he attributed this to the fact of Hindus being in a state of political subjection. "Indeed, in my opinion, at the present moment, we are all predominantly *shudras*, so long as we are serfs" (*ibid.*, p. 9). At another point he attributes this to the fact of *varṇa saṅkara:*

> Owing to the confusion of the *varnas*, today there are in reality no *varnas*, the *varna* principle has

the highest *varṇa* and the process of Sanskritization[12] and *jātyutkarṣa*[13] has been in that direction. But here again Mahatma Gandhi reversed the priorities radically. He called the untouchables *harijans*, God's people,[14] just as a *brāhmaṇa* is one who exhibits Brahma in his life.[15] Nor was the change suggested by him purely terminological, it was substantive. He remarked:

> I regard "Harijan" as a fitting name, because the caste Hindus cannot be properly considered God's children, but the "untouchables"

---

ceased to operate. The present state of Hindu society may be described as that of anarchy; the four *varnas* today exist in name only. If we must talk in terms of *varna*, there is only one *varna* today for all, whether men or women; we are all *shudras* (*ibid.*, p. 343).

12. See M.N. Srinivas, "A Note on Sanskritization and Westernization," *Far Eastern Quarterly*, vol. 15, no. 4 (August, 1956), pp. 481-96. See also Milton Singer, *op. cit.*, *passim*.
13. P.V. Kane, *op. cit.*, vol. II, Part I, pp. 61-66.
14. John R. Hinnells and Eric J. Sharpe, eds., *Hinduism*, *op. cit.*, p. 99: " . . . untouchables whom he renamed Harijans (sons of Hari-Vishnu — God)." More accurately, perhaps, *harijans* should be translated as "people of God" (R.C. Zaehner, *Hinduism* [Oxford University Press, 1966], p. 183). Mahatma Gandhi has sometimes been criticized for being "patronizing" in using the term but it seems that the term was originally proposed to him by some untouchable colleagues, see Rajmohan Gandhi, *Revenge and Reconciliation: Understanding South Asian History* (New Delhi: Penguin Books, 1999), pp. 254-55.
15. M.K. Gandhi, *Hindu Dharma*, p. 350.

> certainly can.[16]

He went on to say:

> I have suggested the real method of abolishing the distinction between caste Hindus and Harijans, namely, by caste Hindus performing the purification ceremony of ridding themselves of untouchability and becoming Harijans themselves. And if it was open to any one to be classified as "untouchables" in the register for "untouchables," I should most decidedly advise caste Hindus to declare themselves as such and to live also as such. That will be a substantial and organic method of amalgamating the two into one body.[17]

In other words, if the caste Hindus are treated as one group and are called *savarṇa*s and the untouchables are treated as a group and called *pañcama*s then in the Hindu religious tradition the *savarṇa*s stood at the top and the *pañcama*s were at the bottom. Mahatma Gandhi was trying to reverse the priority; he was placing the *pañcama*s or Harijans on top, as it were. Once again, Mahatma Gandhi could be seen as making cardinal changes in Hinduism by making ordinal changes within it.[18]

---

16. M.K. Gandhi, *Hindu Dharma*, p. 308.
17. *Ibid.*
18. For more information on Mahatma Gandhi's changing views on the Caste System, see Arvind Sharma, *Modern Hindu Thought: The Essential Texts* (New Delhi: Oxford University Press, 2002), pp. 274-81.

4

Mahatma Gandhi and the Āśrama System

The *āśrama* system is as integral to the Hindu religious tradition, as that of *varṇa*. Indeed, sometimes the expression *varṇāśrama dharma* is used to denote Hinduism:

> We have seen that for the theorist society involved two concepts; one of these was class, or *varṇa,* while the other was stage of life, or *āśrama*. This was a later idea than that of class, and was evidently more artificial. Just as Aryan society was divided into four classes, so the life of the individual Aryan was divided into four stages: on his investiture with the sacred thread, when he put his childhood behind him, he became a *brahmacārin*, leading a celibate and austere life as a student at the home of his teacher; next, having mastered the Vedas, or part of them, he returned to this parental home, and was married, becoming a householder (*gṛhastha*); when, well advanced in middle age, he had seen his children's children and had thus surely established his line, he left his home for the forest to become a hermit (*vānaprastha*); by meditation and penance he freed his soul from material things,

> until at last, a very old man, he left his hermitage and became a homeless wanderer (*sannyāsin*), with all his earthly ties broken.
>
> This scheme, of course, represents the ideal rather than the real. Many young men never passed through the first stage of life in the form laid down, while only a few went beyond the second. Many of the hermits and ascetics of ancient India were not old men, and had either shortened or omitted the stage of householder. The series of the four stages is evidently an idealization of the facts, and an artificial attempt to find room for the conflicting claims of study, family life, and asceticism in a single lifetime. It is possible that the system of the *āśramas* was evolved partly as a counterblast to the unorthodox sects such as Buddhism and Jainism, which encouraged young men to take up asceticism and by-pass family life altogether, a practice which did not receive the approval of the orthodox, though in later times provision was made for it. Despite their artificiality, however, the four stages of life were an ideal which many men in ancient India attempted to follow, and thus they deserve our consideration. Moreover, they serve as a framework round which we can model the life of the individual.[1]

In order to see how Mahatma Gandhi altered the priorities within this scheme it needs to be realized that the Hindu

1. A.L. Basham, *op. cit.*, pp. 159-60.

religious tradition generally upholds the ascetic ideal represented by the life of the *saṁnyāsin*. Although only a small proportion of the Hindus actually become *saṁnyāsins*,[2] those who do or adopt a lifestyle similar to that of one, are held in great veneration. J. Gonda has pointed out that:

> It is because the bhikṣu or the saṁnyāsin embodies this standard of values — in which the moral and spiritual ever have preference over the material — in his own person in the most extreme and striking form, forsaking the world and all its benefits for the spiritual quest, *brahmacarya*, that "the Indian mind perceives in him a symbolic relation to the hoary culture it is heir to."[3]

To see the force the *saṁnyāsin* model exerts on the Hindu mind one need only to observe the number of religious leaders of the Hindu renaissance who conformed to it in varying degrees. Thus Swami Dayananda Sarasvati, Swami Vivekananda and Sri Aurobindo come readily to mind, as also Sri Ramana and Sri Ramakrishna, not to mention the lesser lights such as Narayana Guru and Ramalinga Swami. Mahatma Gandhi, however, did *not* take *saṁnyāsa*. It is true that he observed *brahmacarya* but he did so as a part of the life of a *vānaprastha* and not a *saṁnyāsin*.

---

2. Though this proportion of such world-renouncers may be higher in Indian than in other countries (see A.C. Bouquet, *op. cit.*, pp. 146-47).

3. J. Gonda, *op. cit.*, p. 305.

In his description of the way in which he came to adopt his style of life one should note how he promotes *brahma-carya* but at the same time does not become a *saṁnyāsin* but instead chooses to remain a *vānáprastha*. The passage is a somewhat extended one but is quoted *in toto* in view of its importance.

> What then, I asked myself, should be my relation with my wife? Did my faithfulness consist in making my wife the instrument of my lust? So long as I was the slave of lust, my faithfulness was worth nothing. To be fair to my wife, I must say that she was never the temptress. It was therefore the easiest thing on me to take the vow of *brahmacharya,* if only I willed it. It was my weak will or lustful attachment that was the obstacle.
>
> Even after my conscience had been roused in the matter, I failed twice. I failed because the motive that actuated the effort was none the highest. My main object was to escape having more children. Whilst in England I had read something about contraceptives. I have already referred to Dr. Allinson's birth control propaganda in the chapter on Vegetarianism. If it had some temporary effect on me, Mr. Hill's opposition to those methods and his advocacy of internal effort as opposed to outward means, in a word, of self-control, had a far greater effect, which in due time came to be abiding. Seeing, therefore, that I did not desire more children I began to strive after self-control. There was endless difficulty in the

task. We began to sleep in separate beds. I decided to retire to bed only after the day's work had left me completely exhausted. All these efforts did not seem to bear much fruit, but when I look back upon the past, I feel that the final resolution was the cumulative effect of those unsuccessful strivings.

The final resolution could only be made as late as 1906. Satyagraha had not then been started. I had not the least notion of its coming. I was practising in Johannesburg at the time of the Zulu "Rebellion" in Natal, which came soon after the Boer War. I felt that I must offer my services to the Natal Government on that occasion. The offer was accepted, as we shall see in another chapter. But the work set me furiously thinking in the direction of self-control, and according to my wont I discussed my thoughts with my co-workers. It became my conviction that procreation and the consequent care of children were inconsistent with public service. I had to break up my household at Johannesburg to be able to serve during the "Rebellion." Within one month of offering my services, I had to give up the house I had so carefully furnished. I took my wife and children to Phoenix and led the Indian Ambulance Corps attached to the Natal forces. During the difficult marches that had then to be performed, the idea flashed upon me that I wanted to devote myself to the service of the community in this manner, I must relinquish the desire for children and wealth and live a

> life of a *vanaprastha* — of one retired from household cares.[4]

It may also be added that Mahatma Gandhi looked at *saṁnyāsa* less in terms of the doctrine of the four *āśrama*s and more in terms of the *Bhagavad-Gītā*.[5] He felt that "the meaning of the work *sannyasa*" underwent "in the *Gita*, a transformation. The *sannyasa* of the *Gita* will not tolerate complete cessation of all activity. The *sannyasa* of the *Gita* is all work and yet no work."[6]

Now in opting to live in the world rather than to renounce it and to practice celibacy within marriage, Mahatma Gandhi can be seen as once again making radical ordinal changes. Strictly speaking, *brahmacarya* denotes the first stage of life in a narrow sense but by making it one of his chief concerns in a wider sense he made it represent the last rather than the first stage. *Brahmacarya* is a natural concomitant of *saṁnyāsa* and also of the *vānaprastha* stage but by practising it within the *vānaprastha* stage he conferred a sense of finality on *it* and not on *saṁnyāsa*. In a sense, the first stage was made the last. It may well be a case of compensatory adjustment in the *āśrama* system since as a child-groom he never had a chance to practise *brahmacarya* and leapt straight into the life of a *gṛhastha*.

---

4. M.K. Gandhi, *The Story of My Experiments with Truth*, pp. 253-54.
5. M.K. Gandhi, *Hindu Dharma*, p. 145.
6. *Ibid*. For a comprehensive treatment of these and similar themes see Raghavan N. Iyer, *The Moral and Political Thought of Mahatma Gandhi* (New York: Oxford University Press, 1973).

5

Mahatma Gandhi and the Rāmāyaṇa

As already mentioned in the previous chapter, Mahatma Gandhi altered the priorities, if he did not actually reverse the order of the sources of *dharma* in the Hindu religious tradition. It was also demonstrated how these remarks may also be said to apply to his approach to *varṇāśrama dharma*. But Hindu thought distinguishes between . . .

> The duties . . . those of the castes (*varṇa-dharma*), those of the stages of life (*āśrama-dharma*), and those which are common to all, i.e., cardinal virtues (*sādhāraṇa-dharma*).[1]

The significance of this sense of *dharma*, as standing for *sādhāraṇa dharma* has often been overlooked.[2] In his study of the word *dharma* as used in the Hindu literature, P.V. Kane has drawn attention to its due significance.[3] In the

---

1. T.M.P. Mahadevan, *op. cit.*, p. 69.
2. Two well-known works: *The Wonder that was India* by A.L. Basham and *India in Europe: An Essay in Understanding* by Wilhelm Halbfass, provide striking illustrations of this.
3. "The foregoing brief discussion establishes how the word *dharma* passed through several transitions of meaning

present context of the discussion of the role of Mahatma Gandhi in relation to Hindu *dharma*, it needs to be pointed

---

and how ultimately its most prominent significance came to be 'the privileges, duties and obligations of a man, his standard of conduct as a member of the Āryan community, as a member of one of the castes, as a person in a particular stage of life.' It is in this sense that the word seems to be used in the well-known exhortation to the pupil contained in the Taittirīya Upaniṣad (I.11) 'speak the truth, practice (your own) *dharma* & c.' It is in the same sense that the Bhagavadgītā uses the word *dharma* in the oft-quoted verse '*svadharme nidhanaṁ śreyaḥ*.' The word is employed in this sense in the *dharmaśāstra* literature. The Manusmr̥ti (1.2) tells us that the sages requested Manu to impart instruction in the *dharmas* of all the *varṇas*. The Yajñāvalkya-smr̥ti (I.1) employs it in the same sense. In the Tantra-vārtika also we are told that all the *dharmasūtras* are concerned with imparting instruction in the *dharmas* of *varṇas* and *āśramas*. Medhātithi commenting on Manu says that the expounders of *smr̥tis* dilate upon *dharma* as five-fold, e.g., *varṇa-dharma*, *āśrama-dharma*, *varṇāśrama-dharma*, *naimittikadharma* (such as *prāyaścitta*) and *guṇadharma* (the duty of a crowned king, whether Ksatriya or not, to protect). It may be noted that the Mitākṣarā on Yāj. I.1 after mentioning the fivefold *dharmas* and illustrating them adds a sixth category, viz., '*Sādhāraṇa-dharma*' — duties common to all men (including even *cāṇḍālas*) such as *ahiṁsā* and quotes a vedic passage in support '*na hiṁsyāt sarvā bhūtāni*.' Slightly differing enumerations of virtues to be cultivated by all men are found in Gaut. Dh. S. VIII.23-25, *Matsyapurāṇa* 52.8-10 (8 in all), *Manu* X. 63 (five), *Yaj*. I.1.22 (nine). Vide *H.D.* vol. II pp. 10-11 and vol. V, pp. 1023-24, 1637 and 1648. It may be noted that the Arthaśāstra of Kauṭilya (I.3.13) prescribes for all men *ahiṁsā*, *satya*, *śauca*, *anasuyā*, *ānrśaṁsya* and *kṣamā*. It is

out that the apposition of *varṇāśrama dharma* with *sādhāraṇa dharma* raises the possibility of opposition between the two. The question then arises: in the event of a conflict between the two which *dharma* is to be followed?

Although some writers have tried to argue for the priority of *sādhāraṇa dharma* in such a case on the basis of traditional Hindu ethics, Dr. S.N. Dasgupta maintains that:

> The statement that the common good (*sādhāraṇa-dharma*) could be regarded as the precondition of the specific caste-duties implies that, if the latter came into conflict with the former, then the former should prevail. This is, however, inexact; for there is hardly any instance where, in case of a conflict, the *sādhāraṇa-dharma*, or the common duties, had a greater force. Thus, for example, non-injury to living beings was a common duty; but sacrifices implied the killing of animals, and it was the clear duty of the Brahmins to perform sacrifices. War implied the taking of an immense number of human lives; but it was the duty of a Kṣattriya not to turn away from a battle-field, and in pursuance of his obligatory duty as a Kṣattriya he had to fight. Turning to traditional accounts, we find in the *Rāmāyaṇa* that Śambūka was a Śūdra saint (*muni*) who was performing ascetic penances in a forest. This was a transgression of caste-duties; for a Śūdra could not perform *tapas*,

---

in this sense that the word *dharma* will be taken in this work" (P.V. Kane, *op. cit.*, vol. I, Part I, pp. 3-4).

which only the higher caste people were allowed to undertake, and hence the performance of *tapas* by the Śūdra saint Śambūka was regarded as *adharma* (vice); and, as a result of this *adharma*, there was a calamity in the kingdom of Rāma in the form of the death of infant son of a Brahmin. King Rāma went out in his chariot and beheaded Śambūka for transgressing his caste-duties. Instances could be multiplied to show that, when there was a conflict between the caste-duties and the common duties, it was the former that had the greater force. The common duties had their force only when they were not in conflict with the caste-duties. The *Gītā* is itself an example of how the caste-duties had preference over common duties. In spite of the fact that Arjuna was extremely unwilling to take the lives of his near and dear kinsmen in the battle of Kurukṣetra Kṛṣṇa tried his best to dissuade him from his disinclination to fight and pointed out to him that it was his clear duty, as a Kṣattriya, to fight. It seems therefore very proper to hold that the common duties had only a general application, and that the specific caste-duties superseded them, whenever the two were in conflict.[4]

---

4. P.V. Kane, *op. cit.,* pp. 506-07. It is interesting to note what Mahatma Gandhi has to say about the story of Śambūka, "The story of a shudra having been punished by Ramachandra for daring to learn the Vedas I reject as an interpolation" (M.K. Gandhi, *Hindu Dharma,* p. 9).

Mahatma Gandhi again altered the priorities within the Hindu religious tradition on this point — by giving primacy to *sādhāraṇa dharma* over *varṇāśrama dharma*. Once the following question was put to him:

> In Hinduism devotion of wife to her husband and her complete merger in him is the highest aim, never mind whether the husband is a fiend or an embodiment of love. If this be the correct conduct for a wife, may she in the teeth of opposition by her husband undertake national service? or must she only go so far as the husband will permit her to go?[5]

It need hardly be pointed out that serving the husband is a specific or *viśeṣa dharma*[6] while serving the country is a general or *sādhāraṇa dharma*. He replied:

> My ideal of a wife is Sita and of a husband Rama. But Sita was no slave of Rama. Or each was slave of each other. Rama is ever considerate to Sita. Where there is true love, the question asked does not occur. Where there is no true love, the bond has never existed. But the Hindu household of today is a conundrum. Husbands and wives when they are married know nothing of one another. Religious sanction fortified by custom and the even flow of the lives of the married people keep the peace in the vast majority of Hindu households. But when either wife or husband

5. M.K. Gandhi, *Hindu Dharma*, p. 360.

6. Monier Monier-Williams, *op. cit.*, p. 990.

> holds views out of the ordinary, there is danger of jars. In the case of the husband he has no scruples. He does not consider himself under any obligation to consult his partner's wishes. He regards his wife as his property. And the poor wife who believes in the husband's claim often suppresses herself. I think there is a way out. Mirabai has showed the way. *The wife has a perfect right to take her own course and meekly brave the consequences when she knows herself to be in the right and when her resistance is for a nobler purpose.*[7]

The use of the case of Mīrā as an example is very illuminating. It is well-known that she abandoned her husband and the life of a wife out of intense devotion for Kṛṣṇa. Thus spiritual ends, for Mahatma Gandhi, superseded social commitments related to one's station in life. Similarly morality took precedence over social practices and even over ritual for him. Thus after defining Hinduism as that religion which "tells every one to worship God according to his own faith or *dharma*," he goes on to add:

> That being my conception of Hinduism, I have never been able to reconcile myself to untouchability. I have always regarded it as an excrescence. It is true that it has been handed down to us from generations, but so are many evil practices even to this day. I should be ashamed to think that dedication of girls to virtual prostitution was a part of Hinduism.

7. M.K. Gandhi, *Hindu Dharma*, p. 360, emphasis added.

Yet it is practised by Hindus in many parts of India. I consider it positive irreligion to sacrifice goats to Kali and do not consider it a part of Hinduism. Hinduism is a growth of ages. The very name, Hinduism, was given to the religion of the people of Hindustan by foreigners. There is no doubt at one time sacrifice of animals were offered in the name of religion. But it is not religion, much less is it Hindu religion. And so also it seems to me, that when cow-protection became an article of faith with our ancestors, those who persisted in eating beef were excommunicated. The civil strife must have been fierce. Social boycott was applied not only to the recalcitrants, but their sins were visited upon their children also. The practice which had probably its origin in good intentions hardened into usage, and even verses crept into our sacred books giving the practice a permanence wholly undeserved and still less justified. Whether my theory is correct or not, untouchability is repugnant to reason and to the instinct of mercy, pity or love. A religion that establishes the worship of the cow cannot possibly countenance or warrant a cruel and inhuman boycott of human beings. And I should be content to be torn to pieces rather than disown the suppressed classes. Hindus will certainly never deserve freedom, nor get it, if they allow their noble religion to be disgraced by the retention of the taint of untouchability. And as I love Hinduism dearer than life itself, the taint has become for me an

> intolerable burden. Let us not deny God by denying to a fifth of our race the right of association on an equal footing.[8]

Chastity, mercy and equality are *sādhāraṇa dharma*s; the practice of temple prostitution, sacrifice of animals and the practice of untouchability are *dharma*s of special circumstances. In the event of a conflict between the two it is quite clear from the above passage where Mahatma Gandhi's choice lay.

8. M.K. Gandhi, *Hindu Dharma,* pp. 8-9.

6

Mahatma Gandhi and the Bhagavad-Gītā

A better illustration of Mahatma Gandhi's position on the issue of *sādhārṇa dharma* is provided by his interpretation of the *Bhagavad-Gītā*. As is well known the *Bhagavad-Gītā*

> Takes the form of a dialogue between the prince Arjuna and his charioteer, the god Krishna, whose true nature as an *avatar* of Vishnu gradually becomes apparent. The scene is set on the battlefield of Kuru, where the forces of the five sons of Pandu, (one of whom is Arjuna) are preparing to do battle with their cousins, the sons of Dhritarashtra. Arjuna's nerve suddenly fails him; he is appalled by the fact that he is preparing to slay his kinsmen. He asks Krishna's advice, and is told that it is his duty to fight (he is a *kshatriya*), but the discussion soon moves on to topics that have no direct bearing on this issue. The author of the *Gita* takes up and develops many themes that have already appeared in the Upanishads, and adds to these the notion of *bhakti* (loving

> devotion) — the adoration of God as a means of salvation.[1]

The point to note here is that non-violence or *ahiṁsā* is a *sādhāraṇa dharma* while Arjuna is being asked to engage in combat on the basis of his *varṇa dharma* as a *kṣatriya*. This is at least one way of looking at the situation and in the Gandhian context a very useful one. For in the end Arjuna does consent to fight. Yet Mahatma Gandhi claimed that the message of the *Gītā* was consistent with *ahiṁsā* even though "it may be freely admitted that the *Gita* was not written to establish *ahimsa*."[2] "When the *Gita* was written, although people believed in *ahimsa*, wars were not only not taboo, but nobody observed the contradiction between them and *ahimsa*."[3] Mahatma Gandhi maintained that "It is quite likely that the author did not write it to inculcate *ahiṁsā*, but as a commentator draws innumerable interpretations from a poetic text, even so I interpret the *Gītā* to mean that if its central theme is *anāsakti*, it also teaches *ahiṁsā*."[4] Elsewhere he writes: "I have felt that in trying to enforce in one's life the central teaching of the *Gītā*, one is

---

1. John R. Hinnells and Eric J. Sharpe, eds., *op. cit.*, p. 31, emphasis added. Some scholars would perhaps be less willing to concede that "the discussion soon moves on to topics that have no direct bearing on this issue," for instance, see Thomas J. Hopkins, *The Hindu Religious Tradition* (Belmont, California: Dickenson Publishing Company Inc., 1971), pp. 90-91.
2. M.K. Gandhi, *Hindu Dharma*, p. 144.
3. *Ibid.*, p. 146.
4. *Ibid.*, p. 159, diacritics supplied.

bound to follow truth and *ahiṁsā*."[5] What is important is that he insisted on interpreting the *Gītā* in terms of *sādhāraṇa dharma*. That he should do so with a text so inhospitable to such an interpretation on the face of it only testifies to the decisiveness of Mahatma Gandhi's position that *sādhāraṇa dharma* prevails over any other kind of *dharma*, that *sādhāraṇa dharma* — *satya, ahiṁsā, brahmacarya*, etc., — really represented the *sanātana dharma*.

At this point the question naturally arises: how could Mahatma Gandhi interpret the *Gītā* in such a way? It is important to determine whether Mahatma Gandhi foisted his interpretation on the *Gītā* or whether he saw it as flowing naturally out of the *Gītā*. In other words, how defensible, or even credible, is Mahatma Gandhi's distillation of a *sādhāraṇa dharma* like *ahiṁsā* from a text like the *Gītā* of which it has even been alleged that it was composed to support *varṇāśrama dharma*.[6]

Mahatma Gandhi interpreted the *Bhagavad-Gītā* allegorically.[7] It might be useful to identify the factors that might have led him to do so and their relation to his ethical interpretation of the *Gītā*.

One might begin by considering some general historical or contemporary trends to which Mahatma Gandhi may

---

5. M.K. Gandhi, *Hindu Dharma*, p. 144, diacritics supplied.
6. A.L. Basham, *op. cit.*, pp. 344-45.
7. See M.K. Gandhi, *Hindu Dharma*, pp. 156, 158, 170, 178, etc.; Mahadev Desai, *The Gita According to Gandhi* (Ahmedabad: Navajivan Publishing House, 1956), pp. 135-36 and passim; etc.

have been responding consciously or unconsciously in interpreting the *Gītā* allegorically.

The orthodox exegetical Hindu tradition around the *Gītā* takes the martial setting of the *Gītā* quite literally.[8] One exception to this seems to be suggested by a passage in Abhinavagupta's commentary on the *Gītā*, wherein he cites an alternative explanation according to which the Kurukṣetra represents the human body and the Pāṇḍavas and the Kauravas the forces of Good and Evil respectively.[9] It is highly unlikely however that Mahatma Gandhi would have read it[10] or Raychandbhai for that matter, in whom he came closest to having a spiritual preceptor.[11]

Thus it is highly unlikely that Mahatma Gandhi was a legatee to the tradition of the allegorical interpretation of the *Gītā* through regular Hindu channels. It is more plausible to suggest that he might be responding, in adopting an allegorical approach to the *Gītā*, to a contemporary rather than an ancient trend. W. Douglas P. Hill points out that "many interpreters of the *Gita*, while not denying the

---

8. See Wasudeva Laxmana Shastri Pansikar, ed., *Śrīmad-bhagavadgītā with the Commentaries* (Bombay: Nirnayasagar Press, 1912), pp. 8-10 and *passim*; K.S. Ramaswamy Sastrigal, *The Bhagavadgita with Translation and Notes* (Srirangam: Sri Vani Vilas Press, 1927), pp. 44-46, etc.
9. Wasudeva Laxmana Shastri Pansikar, ed., *op. cit.*, pp. 8-9.
10. Mahatma Gandhi refers to his inadequate knowledge of Sanskrit, see Mahadev Desai, *op. cit.*, pp. 126, 127.
11. M.K. Gandhi, *The Story of My Experiments with Truth*, pp. 113-14. Also see Erik H. Erikson, *Gandhi's Truth* (New York: W.W. Norton & Co.), pp. 162-63.

historicity of the episode, lay greater stress upon its value as allegory."[12] But most of these interpreters are modern. Of the two he mentions by name: Praṇavānanda Svāmin of Benaras[13] and Chhaganlal G. Kaji,[14] the work of one of them postdates Mahatma Gandhi's acquaintance with the *Gītā*, which began in 1888-89. He also mentions Theosophical works, whose influence is more plausible. Their case will be examined in detail later. The other allegorical interpretations of the *Gītā*, such as those by S. Radhakrishnan,[15] come much later. In this respect it should be borne in mind that according to Mahatma Gandhi, "Even in 1888-89, when I first became acquainted with the *Gita* I felt that it was not a historical work."[16] It may also be noted that Edwin Arnold's translation of the *Gītā* which Mahatma Gandhi read[17] does not refer to it as an allegory[18] and that one commentary on the *Gītā* which Mahatma Gandhi refers

---

12. W. Douglas P. Hill, *The Bhagavadgītā* (Oxford University Press, 1928), p. 99.
13. This writer has not succeeded in obtaining a copy of the work or in tracking down any reference to it elsewhere.
14. Chhaganlal G. Kaji, *Philosophy of the Bhagavad Gita: An Exposition* (Rajkot: 1909). For allegorical interpretive tendencies see p. 5, etc.
15. S. Radhakrishnan, *The Bhagavadgītā* (London: George Allen and Unwin Ltd., 1949). For allegorical interpretive tendencies see p. 79, etc.
16. M.K. Gandhi, *Hindu Dharma*, p. 158.
17. M.K. Gandhi, *The Story of My Experiments with Truth*, p. 90.
18. Edwin Arnold, *The Song Celestial* (Boston: Roberts Brothers, 1888), *passim*.

to is the one by Bal Gangadhar Tilak[19] which does not interpret it allegorically; it interprets it activistically. It is very unlikely, therefore, that Mahatma Gandhi adopted an allegorical interpretation of the *Gītā* because this happened to be the vogue.[20]

Thus Mahatma Gandhi's adoption of an allegorical interpretation of the *Gītā* is hard to explain in general terms. Can it be explained in terms of more specific influences?

Robert Payne seems to be of the opinion that it was the character of Edwin Arnold's translation of the *Gītā,* in which Mahatma Gandhi read it for the first time, which led him into interpreting it allegorically:

> Sixty years before, when Gandhi first came upon Sir Edward Arnold's translation of the *Bhagavad Gita* in London, he concluded that it could only have been written about the struggles of the human heart in search of a saviour. Indeed, such an opinion could scarcely be avoided by anyone reading the English translation alone, for the rhythms of the Victorian verse do not permit the reader to see the battle at close quarters. In the original, however, the *Bhagavad Gita* is written in taut, springy couplets almost physical in their impact; the commands of Krishna have an

---

19. Mahadev Desai, *op. cit.*, p. 126.
20. It seems to be in considerable vogue in our own times as well, see A.L. Herman, *The Bhagavad Gītā: A Translation and Critical Commentary* (Springfield: Charles C. Thomas, 1973), pp. 107-08.

> urgency, a kind of paroxysmic fury, which powerfully suggests the utterances of a god in a mood of intense and visionary exaltation; and what he says, in the eyes of most Sanskrit scholars, relates to both heaven and earth, to the world of the spirit and to the battle fought on the plain of Kurukshetra.[21]

This explanation does not appear very convincing. For one thing the description of the metrical effect of the *Bhagavad-Gītā* sounds overblown, at least to this writer. For another, Mahatma Gandhi did ultimately get to read the *Gītā* in the original[22] and thus had a chance to reform his opinion. Besides, Mahatma Gandhi was not guided entirely by his first impression for he tells us that the "preliminary intuition" that it was an allegory "was more confirmed on a closer study of religion and the *Gita*. A study of the *Mahabharata* gave it added confirmation."[23] It should also be kept in mind that Sir Edwin Arnold refers to the Kurukṣetra *only* in geographical terms and describes the scene in realistic terms:

> Its (the Gita's) scene is the level country between the Jumna and the Sarsvoti rivers — now Kurnul and Jheend. Its simple plot consists of a dialogue held by Prince Arjuna, the brother of King Yudhisthira, with Krishna, the Supreme

21. Robert Payne, *The Life and Death of Mahatma Gandhi* (New York: E.P. Dutton, 1969), p. 645.
22. Though with a limited knowledge of Sanskrit, see Mahadev Desai, *op. cit.*, p. 127.
23. M.K. Gandhi, *Hindu Dharma*, p. 158.

> Deity, wearing the disguise of a charioteer. A great battle is impending between the Kauravas and the Pandavas and this conversation is maintained in a war-chariot drawn up between the opposing hosts.[24]

It seems quite unlikely; therefore, that Mahatma Gandhi was predestined to an allegorical interpretation of the *Gītā* by the rhythms of Arnold's translation. What might be more significant is the fact that he read this translation in the company of "two Theosophists, brothers."[25] Was Mahatma Gandhi led to an allegorical interpretation of the *Gītā* under the influence of Theosophy?

This would indeed be quite plausible had he indeed been reading Annie Besant's translation of the *Bhagavad-Gītā* as Agehananda Bharati seems to claim he did;[26] but this does not seem to have been the case as we have seen. Mahatma Gandhi, however, does record the meeting with Mrs. Besant who "had just joined the Theosophical Society and I was following with great interest the controversy about her conversion."[27] Mahatma Gandhi mentions later contacts with her too but the *Gītā* never seems to figure in these accounts.[28] If she had just joined the Society it is highly unlikely that her translation, which is definitely headed

24. Edwin Arnold, *op. cit.*, p. 9.
25. M.K. Gandhi, *The Story of My Experiments with Truth*, p. 90.
26. Agehananda Bharati, "The Hindu Renaissance and its Apologetic Patterns," *The Journal of Asian Studies*, vol. XXIX, no. 2, February 1970, pp. 274-75.
27. M.K. Gandhi, *The Story of My Experiments with Truth*, p. 91.
28. *Ibid.*, pp. 92, 293, 298, 538, 546, 610.

towards an allegorical interpretation,[29] would have been in print.[30] Mahatma Gandhi does, however, "recall having read, at the brothers' instance, Madame Blavatsky's *Key to Theosophy.*"[31] Could this book have influenced Mahatma Gandhi towards an allegorical interpretation of the *Gītā*? The possibility exists but the book contains only two references to the *Bhagavad-Gītā* which in themselves do not imply allegorization.[32] Thus on the whole it is hard to account for the allegorization of the *Gītā* by Mahatma Gandhi in terms of Theosophical influences.

At this point in the investigation it will be helpful to recognize that the allegorical interpretation of the *Gītā* is a logical corollary to the Gandhian claim that the *Bhagavad-Gītā* preaches non-violence. Hence it could be maintained that Mahatma Gandhi interpreted the *Gītā* allegorically because of his commitment to the doctrine of non-violence. And if he adopted the doctrine of *ahiṁsā* under either Jaina

29. Annie Besant, *The Bhagavadgita* (London: Theosophical Publishing Society, 1904), Preface. The tendency is even more marked in her *Hints on the Study of the Bhagavad-Gita* (London: Theosophical Publishing Society, 1906).

30. The earliest date on Annie Besant's translation of the *Bhagavadgita* this writer has been able to trace seems to be 1895.

31. M.K. Gandhi, *The Story of My Experiments with Truth,* p. 91. He adds: "This book stimulated in me a desire to read books on Hinduism and disabused me of the notion fostered by the missionaries that Hinduism was rife with superstition" (*ibid.*).

32. H.P. Blavatsky, *The Key to Theosophy* (London: Theosophical Publishing Society, 1889), pp. 49, 67n.

or Christian influence then the allegorization of the *Gītā* might be traced to these influences, though at one remove.

Mahatma Gandhi personally attests to the fact that "Jainism was strong in Gujarat, and its influence was felt everywhere and on all occasions."[33] It is well known that Jainism emphasizes *ahiṁsā* even more than Hinduism and Buddhism.[34] Moreover, Jainism could also have been directly responsible for an allegorical interpretation of the *Gītā* by Mahatma Gandhi for it is well known that Jaina scholars often offer rational explanations for Hindu myths.[35] Was then Jaina influence responsible for an allegorical interpretation of the *Gītā* either directly or indirectly?

The specific direction which Jaina influence seems to have assumed early in the case of Mahatma Gandhi seems to have been vegetarianism as an expression of non-violence.[36] On the doctrinal aspects of *ahiṁsā*, however, there seem to have been differences between the Jaina and Gandhian positions as is clear from the "calf-controversy,"[37] and the "rabid-dog incident."[38] Thus one should not

33. M.K. Gandhi, *The Story of My Experiments with Truth*, pp. 33-34.
34. See A.L. Basham, ed., *A Cultural History of India* (Oxford: Clarendon Press, 1975), pp. 109-10.
35. See Maurice Winternitz, *A History of Indian Literature*, vol. II (University of Calcutta, 1933), pp. 490-91.
36. M.K. Gandhi, *The Story of My Experiments with Truth*, pp. 33-34.
37. See Robert Payne, *op. cit.*, pp. 381-82.
38. Erik H. Erikson, *op. cit.*, pp. 422-23. But elsewhere Gandhi opposes killing of venomous reptiles, see M.K. Gandhi, *Hindu Dharma*, *op. cit.*, p. 151.

overestimate the probability of Jaina influence, especially as the Mahatma himself was conscious of these differences.[39] As a matter of fact, on the more specific issue of the *Bhagavad-Gītā* and non-violence with which we are concerned here, Mahatma Gandhi clearly states, his non-violent interpretation of the text notwithstanding, "Not that actual physical battle is out of the question. To those who are innocent of non-violence the *Gita* does not teach a lesson of despair. . . . Better than cowardice is killing and being killed in battle."[40] This may be contrasted with the Jaina account in which Kṛṣṇa goes to hell for preaching violence to Arjuna! Moreover, while Jaina scholars do "rationalize" some Hindu myths the fact of the *Mahābhārata* war never seems to have been doubted.[41] As a matter of fact, Jaina accounts make "Vāsudeva-Kṛṣṇa a contemporary of Tirthankara Arishṭanemi, who preceded Pārśavanātha."[42] The attribution of the allegorical interpretation of the *Gītā* by Mahatma Gandhi to Jaina influence is therefore full of difficulties.

But what about Christian influences? Mahatma Gandhi himself observed that "My interpretation of the *Gita* has been criticized by orthodox scholars as being unduly

39. See M.K. Ghandhi, *Hindu Dharma*, p. 227 ff.

40. *Ibid.*, p. 156.

41. See Joseph W. Elder, ed., *Chapters in Indian Civilization*, vol. 1, (Iowa: Kendall/Hunt Publishing Co., 1970), p. 79.

42. See Jina Vinaya Muni, ed., *The Jains in the History of Indian Literature by Dr. Maurice Winternitz* (Ahmedabad: Jaina Sahitya Samsodhaka Pratisthan, 1946), pp. 6, 10, 12, 17, etc.

influenced by the Sermon on the Mount"[43] and Robert Payne adds, "it was no more than the truth."[44] Will Durant notes how his critics "consider him not a Hindu but a Christian; they quote his favourite book, the *Bhagavad-Gita*, to show him that Hinduism counsels not non-violence but active striking, "natural killing" for a good cause. At the Delhi Conference a Hindu rose and said: "I oppose this non-violence, this non-cooperation. I ask you, is it Hindu teaching? It is not. Is it Mohammedan teaching? It is not. I will tell you what it is. It is Christian."[45] Thus it could be argued that the allegorical interpretation of the *Gītā* was resorted to by Mahatma Gandhi to reconcile it with the *New Testament*. Apart from this indirect influence one could also argue that Mahatma Gandhi's allegorization could be the result of direct Christian missionary influence, for the Christian missionaries and some Western scholars as well, had cast doubt on the historicity of several Hindu gods and heroes.

On closer inspection, however, the case for Christian influence as explaining the allegorization of the *Gītā* by Mahatma Gandhi does not seem to be very strong. It is true that Mahatma Gandhi says the Sermon on the Mount went straight to his heart.[46] But it appealed to him not because

43. R.C. Majumdar, ed., *The Age of Imperial Unity* (Bombay: Bharatiya Vidya Bhavan, 1968), p. 434. Also see A.L. Basham, ed., *op. cit.*, pp. 100-01.

44. Quoted by Robert Payne, *op. cit.*, p. 645.

45. Will Durant, *The Case for India* (New York: Simon and Shuster, 1930), p. 105.

46. Mahatma Gandhi, *The Story of My Experiments with Truth*, p. 92.

of its originality but because of its conformity to what he had already learnt. For long ago a "Gujarati didactic stanza" had "gripped" his "mind and heart" and "its precept return good for evil" had become Mahatma Gandhi's guiding principle.[47] Mahatma Gandhi refers to that stanza of Shamal Bhatt in recording his reactions to reading the *New Testament*:

> But the New Testament produced a different impression, especially the Sermon on the Mount which went straight to my heart. I compared it with the *Gita*. The verses, "But I say unto thee, that ye resist not evil: but whoever shall smite thee on thy right cheek, turn to him the other also. And if any take away thy coat let him have thy cloak too" delighted me beyond measure and put me in mind of Shamal Bhatt's "For a bowl of water, give a goodly meal," etc.[48]

So far as the direct influence of the Christian attack on the historicity of Hindu figures is considered, it should be noted that Mahatma Gandhi, while he may have regarded them as allegorical, did not necessarily regard them as mythical. This is clear from his treatment of Kṛṣṇa.

> Krishna in the *Gita* is perfection and right knowledge personified; but the picture is imaginary. *That does not mean that Krishna, the adored of his people, never lived.* But perfection is

47. Mahatma Gandhi, *The Story of My Experiments with Truth*, p. 51.

48. *Ibid.*, p. 92. Also see Erik H. Erikson, *op. cit.*, p. 151.

> imagined. The idea of a perfect incarnation is an after growth.[49]

At this point one has to face a basic biographical fact about Mahatma Gandhi's life. It is this. It was mentioned above that an allegorical interpretation of the *Gītā* is the logical corollary to the claim that it preaches non-violence; logical yes, but not chronological. That is to say, in Mahatma Gandhi's case the view that the *Gītā* is allegorical precedes his commitment to non-violence and his conclusion that it preaches *ahiṁsā*. For he says clearly that,

> Even in 1888-89, when I first became acquainted with the *Gita*, I felt that it was not a historical work, but that under the guise of physical warfare, it described the duel that perpetually went on in the hearts of mankind, and that physical warfare was merely brought in to make the description of the internal duel more alluring.[50]

But what was the extent of Mahatma Gandhi's commitment to *ahiṁsā* in 1888-89? Fortunately we have an autobiographical testament from the Mahatma which answers the question:

---

49. M.K. Gandhi, *Hindu Dharma*, p. 159, emphasis added. Elsewhere too Mahatma Gandhi accepts this about the *Mahābhārata* that the "persons described therein may be historical" but emphasizes the point that "the author of the *Mahabharata* has used them merely to drive home his religious theme" (*ibid.*, p. 158).

50. *Ibid.*

> My first acquaintance with the *Gita* was in 1889, when I was almost twenty. I had not then much of an inkling of the principle of *ahimsa*. One of the lines of the Gujarati poet, Shamalbhatta, had taught me the principle of winning even the enemy with love, and that teaching had gone deep into me. But I had not deduced the eternal principle of non-violence from it. . . . I believed in those days for preparing ourselves for a fight with the English.[51]

This biographical fact — that Mahatma Gandhi's view that the *Gītā* is to be interpreted allegorically precedes his wholehearted commitment to *ahiṁsā* — is an important analytical consequence. One can no longer maintain, as was suggested earlier, that the latter may have been responsible for the former. Mahatma Gandhi's position that the *Gītā* is an allegory must be analysed on its own terms.

Thus when the issue is faced on its own terms the key factor which led Mahatma Gandhi towards an allegorical interpretation of the *Gītā* seems to be what he calls "internal evidence."[52] For Mahatma Gandhi the cumulative effect of these pieces of internal evidence clearly established his case for an allegorical interpretation of the *Bhagavad-Gītā*. The following bits of "internal evidence," it seems, played a key role in leading Mahatma Gandhi in the direction he went.

---

51. M.K. Gandhi, *Hindu Dharma*, p. 151.

52. Mahatma Gandhi wrote in 1936: "The *Mahabharata* and the *Ramayana*, the two books that millions of Hindus know and regard as their guides, are undoubtedly allegories as the internal evidence shows," (*ibid.*, p. 178, emphasis added).

(1) Mahatma Gandhi maintained that if one takes the *Mahābhārata* as a whole, of which the *Gītā* "is a small portion,"[53] "the author of the *Mahābhārata* has not established the necessity of physical warfare; on the contrary he has proved its futility. He has made the victors shed tears of sorrow and repentance and has left them nothing but a legacy of miseries."[54] Thus it would be misleading to take the *Mahābhārata* as emphasizing physical warfare.

(2) The Ādiparva is the first of the eighteen *parva*s of the *Mahābhārata*. According to Mahatma Gandhi "The Adiparva contains powerful evidence in support of my opinion. By ascribing to the chief actors superhuman or subhuman origins, the great Vyasa made short work of the history of kings and their people."[55] In other words, the author wanted to move from history to allegory.

(3) Turning next to the *Bhagavad-Gītā* itself "the crown" "of the great work,"[56] the *Mahābhārata*, Mahatma Gandhi points out that "after the first mention of fighting, there is no mention of fighting at all. The rest is a spiritual discourse,"[57] thus making the

53. M.K. Gandhi, *Hindu Dharma*, p. 168.

54. *Ibid.*, p. 140, diacritics supplied.

55. *Ibid.*

56. *Ibid.*

57. *Ibid.*, p. 158.

allegorical interpretation all the more plausible.[58]

(4) Next to the chapters of the *Bhagavad-Gītā*, Mahatma Gandhi's understanding of it is dominated by the second chapter[59] and here too by the "19 verses at the close of the second chapter."[60] This fact seems to be crucial to understanding why Mahatma Gandhi was led specifically towards an allegorical explanation of the *Gita* apart from his more general accounts, a text which each age must read in the light of its spiritual knowledge.[61]

The significance of those verses can be seen from the fact that when Mahatma Gandhi speaks of his initial

---

58. It is not entirely correct to say that after the first mention of fighting there is no mention of it at all. But though the statement is not entirely accurate it perhaps conveys the correct impression. S.C. Roy observes that "in thirteen out of eighteen chapters of the *Gītā* (viz., Chap. IV-X and Chap. XII-XVII) we do not meet with a single reference to the scene of the battlefield of Kurukṣetra, nor to the Epic story, or incidents of any kind, which might remind us of the fact that Kr̥ṣṇa and Arjuna had anything to do with the Bhārata war or that the object of the teachings of the *Gītā* was to induce Arjuna to fight, so preoccupied and deeply absorbed are both speakers of the dialogue in topics relating to modes of spiritual culture, the ethical ideal and subtle metaphysical concepts" (*The Bhagavadgītā and Modern Scholarship*) [London: Luzac & Co., 1941], pp. 146-47).

59. M.K. Gandhi, *Hindu Dharma,* p. 159.

60. *Ibid.,* p. 179.

61. Ainslie T. Embree, ed., *The Hindu Tradition* (New York: Vintage Books, 1972), p. 339.

acquaintance with the *Gītā* through Edwin Arnold's translation, he observes that they "made a deep impression on my mind, and they still ring in my ears."[62]

Then again, he wrote in the *Young India* in 1931, that the second chapter of the *Gītā*:

> . . . instead of teaching the rules of physical warfare, tells us how a perfected man is to be known. In the characteristics of the perfected man of the *Gita*, I do not see any to correspond to physical warfare. The whole design is inconsistent with the rules governing the relation between warring parties.[63]

Again in 1939 he confronted Dr. Kagawa, "a student of religion" with the same argument:

> The message of the *Gita* is to be found in the second chapter of the *Gita* where Krishna speaks of the balanced state of mind, of mental equipoise. In 19 verses at the close of the 2nd chapter of the *Gita*, Krishna explains how this state can be achieved. It can be achieved, he tells us, after killing all your passions. It is not possible to kill your brother after having killed all your passions. I should like to see that man dealing death — who has no passions, who is indifferent to pleasure and pain, who is undisturbed by the storms that trouble mortal man. The whole thing is described in language of beauty that is unsurpassed. These verses

62. M.K. Gandhi, *The Story of My Experiments with Truth,* p. 90.
63. M.K. Gandhi, *Hindu Dharma,* p. 159.

> show that the fight Krishna speaks of is a spiritual fight.[64]

To conclude: it was neither general exegetical currents, historical or contemporary; nor the nature of Edwin Arnold's translation *per se*; nor Theosophical, Jaina or Christian influences; nor the doctrine of *ahiṁsā* in general which led Mahatma Gandhi towards an allegorical interpretation of the *Bhagavad-Gītā*. What led him in that direction was what he regarded as "internal evidence in support of this interpretation . . . in the work itself and in the *Mahabharata* of which the *Gita* is a minute part."[65]

64. M.K. Gandhi, *Hindu Dharma*, p. 158.

65. *Ibid.*, p. 179. See also p. 154.

7

Mahatma Gandhi and Sādhāraṇa Dharma

The analysis of Mahatma Gandhi's position on untouchability furthered our understanding of how and perhaps even why Mahatma Gandhi altered if not reversed the priorities in relation to the four sources of *dharma*, and the four orders called *varṇa*s. Similarly, an analysis of his motives for undertaking *brahmacarya* furthered our understanding of how and perhaps even why Mahatma Gandhi modified, if he did not reverse, the priorities in relation to the four stages of life called *āśrama*s. Now an analysis of how Mahatma Gandhi arrived at his interpretation of the *Gītā* seems to have furthered our understanding of how, if not why, Mahatma Gandhi gave primacy to *sādhāraṇa dharma*s over *varṇāśrama dharma*.

The *sādhāraṇa-dharma*s are *dharma*s which are common to all *varṇa*s or all the people as "Goodness is not the property of any class or community. The Hindu Scriptures give several lists of virtues."[1] In the *Manu-Smṛti*, for instance, the following list is found:

---

1. T.M.P. Mahadevan, *op. cit.*, p. 79.

> Abstention from injuring (creatures), veracity, abstention from unlawfully appropriating (the goods of others), purity, and control of the organs, Manu has declared to be the summary of the law for the four castes.[2]

The *sādhāraṇa dharmas* thus represent the general principles of an uplifting moral and spiritual life. For Mahatma Gandhi three such virtues seems to have been pre-eminent: Truth (*satya*),[3]

---

2. Sarvepalli Radhakrishnan and Charles A. Moore, eds., *op. cit.*, p. 175. The *sādhāraṇa dharmas* are also common to the various *āśramas*. Manu says (*ibid.*):

> By twice-born men belonging to (any of) these four orders, the tenfold law must be ever carefully obeyed.
>
> Contentment, forgiveness, self-control, abstention from unrighteously appropriating anything, (obedience to the rules of) purification, coercion of the organs [control of the senses], wisdom, knowledge (of the supreme Self), truthfulness, and abstention from anger (form) the tenfold law.
>
> — VI.87-92

3. "The word *satya* (Truth) is derived from *Sat* which means 'being.' Nothing is or exists in reality except Truth. That is why *Sat* or Truth is perhaps the most important name of God. In fact it is more correct to say that Truth is God, than to say that God is Truth. But as we cannot do without a ruler or a general, names of God such as 'King of Kings' or 'the Almighty' are and will remain generally current. On deeper thinking, however, it will be realized, that *Sat* or *Satya* is the only correct and fully significant name for God.

Non-violence (*ahiṁsā*)[4] and celibacy or chastity (*brahma-*

And where there is Truth, there also is knowledge which is true. Where there is no Truth, there can be no true knowledge. That is why the word *Chit* or knowledge is associated with the name of God. And where there is true knowledge, there is always bliss (*Ananda*). There sorrow has no place. And even as Truth is eternal, so is the bliss derived from it. Hence we know God as Sat-chit-ananda, One who combines in Himself Truth, Knowledge and Bliss.

Devotion to this Truth is the sole justification for our existence. All our activities should be centered in Truth. Truth should be the very breath of our life. When once this stage in the pilgrim's progress is reached, all other rules of correct living will come without effort, and obedience to them will be instinctive. But without Truth it would be impossible to observe any principles or rules in life" (M.K. Gandhi, *Hindu Dharma,* p. 221).

4. "*Ahimsa* is not the crude thing it has been made to appear. Not to hurt any living thing is no doubt a part of *ahimsa*. But it is its least expression. The principle of *ahimsa* is hurt by every evil thought, by undue haste, by lying, by hatred, by wishing ill to anybody. It is also violated by our holding on to what the world needs. But the world needs even what we eat day by day. In the place where we stand there are millions of micro-organisms to whom the place belongs, and who are hurt by our presence there. What should we do then? Should we commit suicide? Even that is no solution, if we believe, as we do, that so long as the spirit is attached to the flesh, on every destruction of the body it weaves for itself another. The body will cease to be only when we give up all attachment to it. This freedom from all attachment is the realization of God as Truth. Such realization cannot be attained in a hurry. The body does not belong to us. While it

carya).[5] Not only were these pre-eminent, they were also inseparable. As Jan Gonda has remarked:

---

lasts, we must use it as a trust handed over to our charge. Treating it in this way the things of the flesh, we must strive day by day towards the ideal with what strength we have in us.

It is perhaps clear from the foregoing, that without *ahimsa* it is not possible to seek and find Truth. *Ahimsa* and Truth are so intertwined that it is practically impossible to disentangle and separate them. They are like the two sides of a coin, or rather of a smooth unstamped metallic disc. Who can say, which is the obverse, and which is the reverse? Nevertheless *ahimsa* is the means; Truth is the end. Means to be means must always be within our reach, and so *ahimsa* is our supreme duty. If we take care of the means, we are bound to reach the end sooner or later. When once we have grasped this point, final victory is beyond question. Whatever difficulties we encounter, whatever apparent reverses we sustain, we may not give up the quest for Truth which alone is, being God Himself" (*ibid.*, pp. 224-25).

5. "The third among our observances is *brahmacharya*. As a matter of fact all observances are deducible from Truth, and are meant to subserve it. The man, who is wedded to Truth and worships Truth alone, proves unfaithful to her, if he applies his talents to anything else. How then can he minister to the senses? A man, whose activities are wholly consecrated to the realization of Truth, which requires utter selflessness, can have no time for the selfish purpose of begetting children and running a household. Realization of Truth through self-gratification should, after what has been said before, appear a contradiction in terms.

If we look at it from the standpoint of *ahimsa* (non-violence), we find that the fulfilment of *ahimsa* is impossible without

. . . Attaching the utmost value to the three

---

utter selflessness. *Ahimsa* means Universal Love. If a man gives his love to one woman, or a woman to one man, what is there left for all the world besides? It simply means, We two first, and the devil take the rest of them. As a faithful wife must be prepared to sacrifice her all for the sake of her husband, and a faithful husband for the sake of his wife, it is clear that such persons cannot rise to the height of Universal Love, or look upon all mankind as kith and kin. For they have created a boundary wall round their love. The larger their family, the farther are they from Universal Love. Hence one who would obey the law of *ahimsa* cannot marry, not speak of gratification outside the marital bond" (*ibid.*, p. 225).

J. Gonda remarks thus on Mahatma Gandhi's concept of *brahmacarya*: "It may finally be of interest to quote some passages from Mahatma Gandhi's remarks on this subject. . . . 'My meaning of brahmacarya is this: "One who has never had any lustful intention, who by constant attendance to God, has become capable of lying naked with naked women, however beautiful they may be, without being in any manner whatsoever sexually excited: such a person should be incapable of lying, incapable of doing harm to a single man or woman, free from anger and malice and detached in the sense of the *Gītā*." ' These words written towards the end of his life are in accordance with Gandhi's explanation of the vows to be observed in his Satyagraha Asram in the year 1915: 'it is wellnigh impossible to observe the vows of truth (*satya*) and of ahimsa unless "celibacy" (*brahmacarya-*) is also observed: one has so to control one's animal passions that they will not be moved even in thought.' Knowing the vicious dissipation of energy entailed by the unbridled pursuit of lust he made, in the year 1926, an attempt to be more explicit: 'If abstinence is practiced

great virtues of truth (*satya*), *ahiṁsā* and *brahmacarya,* Gandhi considered Truth — which he identified with God — inseparable from the

---

with the desire to strengthen the bond of love, to purify it, to conserve the vital energy for a better purpose . . ., it will promote equanimity, and strengthen the bond of affection. . . . Marriage must be considered as a sacrament imposing discipline upon the partners, restricting them to the physical union only for the purpose of procreation. . . . The observance of the law of continence is impossible without a living faith in God, which is living Truth.' Without brahmacarya all education will come to naught. Avoiding lustful contact with women is only the beginning. The perfection is reached when the brahmacari refuses to be ruffled or angry, no matter what provocation is offered to him. For anger is the destruction of *virya*, the vital essence. Understanding that the etymological sense of the term gives the clue to the purpose for which this virtue was ordained Gandhi observed: 'Attainment of brahmacarya in the sense here meant means mastery of the science of life.' 'He is a true brahmacari who does not fritter away his energy. He will therefore always control his speech.' 'What is brahmacarya? It is the way of life which leads us to Brahma (God). It includes full control over the process of reproduction. The control must be in thought, word, and deed. If the thought is not under control, the other two have no value. . . . The brahmacari of my conception will be healthy and will easily live long. . . . Mental and physical work will not cause fatigue. . . . He will exhibit all the attributes of the steadfast one described in the Gita. . . . It is strange that one who is able completely to conserve and sublimate the vital fluid which has the potentiality of creating human beings, should exhibit all the attributes described above?' " (*op. cit.*, pp. 312-13).

two other virtues, viz., universal love and self-restraint in all things.[6]

---

6. *op. cit.*, p. 312. R.C. Zaehner observes similarly if somewhat more critically that, "Truth, *ahimsa*, and *brahmacarya* (continence) are the three great virtues that presided over Gandhi's life. Unlike the Advaitins he did not claim to know Absolute Truth, but he did claim to know that God is Truth and that Truth is God; and by truth he understood being true to oneself and to the inner light that is our conscience. Thus he did not hesitate to say that atheism sincerely believed in the atheist's truth. He was, however, not so naïve as to suppose that conscience is necessarily infallible; it can be warped not only by false views but by wrong living. Truth is therefore inseparable from *ahimsa* and *brahmacarya* — the 'harmlessness' that is yet a positive and universal love, and self-restraint in all things, in eating and drinking as much as in sexual relations.

   Gandhi's views on sexuality were quite as strict as were those of Ramakrishna, for as a young man he had not been a stranger to lust and he knew the vicious dissipation of energy that its unbridled pursuit entails. Of the unmarried he demanded total continence, while for the married he considered that intercourse was allowable for the purpose of procreation only. If one did not want a large family, then one had only to exercise self-restraint. As to contraception it was an abomination. 'He condemns sexual life as inconsistent with the moral progress of man,' Rabindranath Tagore wrote, 'and has a horror of sex as great as that of the author of *The Kreutzer Sonata*, but, unlike Tolstoy, he betrays no abhorrence of the sex that tempts his kind. In fact, his tenderness for women is one of the noblest and most consistent traits of his character and he counts among the women of his country some of the best and truest comrades in the great movement he is leading.'

The practice of these virtues constituted the main vows[7] in Mahatma Gandhi's *āśramas*:

> The trinity of virtues on which all other virtues depend — truth, *ahiṁsā*, and *brahmacarya* — naturally formed the cornerstone on which the ashram's life was based, the two latter being the indispensable *practical* pre-condition of the former.[8]

As pointed out earlier, Mahatma Gandhi gave overriding priority to these general moral virtues over other obligations and duties which may be lumped as *varṇāśrama dharmas*. The cardinal significance of this ordinal reversal is best illustrated by the use of *ahiṁsā* as a weapon in the national struggle for Indian Independence.[9] The *Gītā*, wherein

---

To find the truth within oneself one needs to practise the negative virtue of *brahmacarya*. *Brahmacarya*, 'faring according to Brahman,' in practice means total self-control, and Gandhi saw that the etymology of the word gives the clue to the purpose for which this virtue was ordained: it is the highroad of *dharma* that leads to *moksha*" (*op. cit.*, p. 175).

7. The full list consists of the following: Truth, Non-violence, Chastity, Non-possession, Control of the Palate, Non-stealing, Fearlessness, Removal of Untouchability, Bread Labour, Equality of Religions and Swadeshi (see M.K. Gandhi, *Hindu Dharma*, p. 220).

8. R.G. Zaehner, *op. cit.*, p. 182.

9. This interpretation, which sees in the adoption of non-violent means of a struggle against the British the supersession of *viśeṣa-dharma* by *sādhāraṇa dharma*, differs from the interpretation offered by some scholars who see in the adoption of a

Arjuna fought with weapons, may be contrasted with the following scene of non-violent struggle which we owe to

---

non-violent strategy by Mahatma Gandhi traces of his own *varṇa-dharma* at work. Thus R.C. Zaehner comments:

> Yudhishthira was a Kshatriya in violent revolt against the *dharma* of his class. He was pitted against the usurping power of his cousins, the Kauravas, and he was prepared to go to the limit in making concessions; and it was only when all else had failed and the Kauravas wished to deny him even five villages in which he might reign that, spurred on by Krishna, he plunged into bloody war. From the depths of his soul he hated the war, and after it was over accepted in bitter anguish responsibility for the carnage of which he was in fact innocent. Gandhi was a member of the Vaiśya class, and warfare was therefore in no way part of his duties; but circumstances and his own conscience forced him to declare non-violent war on the Kshatriyas of his time, the British Government in India. Yudhishthira had in the end and against his will to resort to arms because that was the *dharma* of his class; Gandhi was under no such obligation. He had hoped to conduct the struggle entirely by non-violent means, but even he, in the end, could not curb the unreasoning fury of the masses: non-violence gave way to violence, and this for Gandhi spelt spiritual defeat. Just as Yudhishthira, after the conclusion of a triumphant war, could not rid himself of the feeling of guilt and responsibility, so did Gandhi take full responsibility for the eruption of violence that his Civil

an American eye-witness. Mr. Webb Miller, Foreign Correspondent of the United Press, U.S.A., describes the events of 21 May, 1930 during the Salt Satyāgraha at Dharasana thus:

> Mme. Naidu called for prayer before the march started and the entire assemblage knelt. She exhorted them: "Gandhi's body is in jail but his soul is with you. India's prestige is in your hands, you must not use any violence under any circumstances. You will be beaten but you must not resist; you must not even raise a hand to ward off blows." Wild, shrill cheers terminated her speech.
>
> Slowly and in silence the throng commenced the half-mile march to salt-deposits. A few carried ropes for lassoing the barbed-wire stockade around the salt pans. About a score who were assigned to act as stretcher-bearers wore crude, hand-painted red crosses pinned to their breasts, their stretchers consisted of blankets. Manilal Gandhi, second son of Gandhi, walked among the foremost of the marchers. As the throng drew near the salt

---

> Disobedience campaign had led to and against which he protested with all his soul. (*op. cit.*, p. 172).

The fact which seems to have been overlooked here is that at one stage in his life Mahatma Gandhi was quite willing to see the British expelled through the use of physical force (see M.K. Gandhi, *Hindu Dharma*, p. 134).

pans they commenced chanting the revolutionary slogans, *Inquilab Zindabad,* intoning the two words over and over.

The salt-deposits were surrounded by ditches filled with water and guarded by four hundred native Surat Police in Khaki shorts and brown turbans. Half a dozen British officials commanded them. The Police carried *lathis* — five foot clubs tipped with steel. Inside the stockade twenty-five native rifle-men were drawn up.

In complete silence the Gandhi men drew up and halted a hundred yards from the stockade. A picked column advanced from the crowd, waded the ditches, and approached the barbed-wire stockade, which the Surat Police surrounded, holding clubs at the ready. Police officials ordered the marchers to disperse under a recently imposed regulation which prohibited gathering of more than five persons in any one place. The column silently ignored the warning and slowly walked forward. I stayed with the main body about a hundred yards from the stockade.

Suddenly, at a word of command, scores of native police rushed upon the advancing marchers and rained blows on their heads with their steel-shod *lathi*s. Not one of the marchers even raised an arm to fend off the blows. They went down like tenpins. From where I stood I heard the sickening whacks of the clubs on unprotected skulls. The waiting crowd of watchers groaned and sucked in their breath in sympathetic pain at every blow.

Those struck down fell sprawling, unconscious or writhing in pain with fractured skulls or broken shoulders. In two or three minutes the ground was quilted with bodies. Great patches of blood widened on their white clothes. The survivors, without breaking ranks, silently and doggedly marched on until struck down, stretcher-bearers rushed up unmolested by the Police and carried off the injured to a thatched hut which had been arranged as a temporary hospital.

Then another column formed while the leaders pleaded with them to retain their self-control. They marched slowly towards the police. Although everyone knew that within a few minutes he would be beaten down, perhaps killed, I could detect no signs of wavering or fear. They marched steadily with heads up, without the encouragement of music or cheering or any possibility that they might escape serious injury or death. The police rushed out and methodically and mechanically beat down the second column. There was no fight, no struggle; the marchers simply walked forward until struck down. There were no outcries, only groans after they fell. There were not enough stretcher-bearers to carry off the wounded; I saw eighteen injured being carried off simultaneously, while forty-two still lay

> bleeding on the ground awaiting stretcher-bearers. The blankets used as stretchers were sodden with blood.[10]

It has been said that "Gandhi did not let Hinduism go: but after Gandhi Hinduism will never be the same again."[11] Yet in one crucial respect Mahatma Gandhi did not let go of Hinduism. Even though one may draw "no line of demarcation between salvation and worldly pursuits"[12] in the spirit of the *Gītā*, or say "in all humility, that those who say that religion has nothing to do with politics do not know what religion means,"[13] yet the goal of human life for Mahatma Gandhi remained the attainment of *mokṣa*. Mahatma Gandhi may have reversed the priorities in the order of the sources of *dharma*, of the *varṇa*s, of the *āśrama*s and of the relationship between *varṇāśrama* and *sādhāraṇa dharma* but he did not either alter the interpretation of the *trivarga* in Hinduism — that *dharma*, *artha* and *kāma* represent a descending scale of values[14] or the fact that the fourth *puruṣārtha* — that of *mokṣa* — represents the final

---

10. See R.C. Majumdar, ed., *Struggle for Freedom* (Bombay: Bharatiya Vidya Bhavan, 1969) pp. 471-72. For the philosophical implications of this see Joan V. Bondurant, *The Conquest of Violence: The Gandhian Philosophy of Conflict* (Princeton, New Jersey: Princeton University Press, 1958).
11. R.C. Zaehner, *op. cit.*, p. 185.
12. M.K. Gandhi, *Hindu Dharma*, p. 144.
13. M.K. Gandhi, *The Story of My Experiments with Truth*, p. 615.
14. Wm. Theodore de Bary, ed., *Sources of Indian Tradition* (Columbia University Press, 1958) Chapter IX *passim*, especially p. 209.

ascension — the supreme end of human life — the *parama puruṣārtha.*[15]

> What I want to achieve — what I have been striving and pinning to achieve these thirty years, — is self-realization, to see God face to face, to attain Moksha. I live and move and have my being in pursuit of this goal. All that I do by way of speaking and writing, and all my ventures in the political field, are directed to this same end.[16]

---

15. Wm. Theodore de Bary, ed., *Sources of Indian Tradition* (Columbia University Press, 1958) Chapter IX *passim*, especially p. 271.

16. M.K. Gandhi, *The Story of My Experiments with Truth*, pp. 4-5. For more on Mahatma Gandhi's religious thought see Margaret Chatterjee, *Gandhi's Religious Thought* (London: The MacMillan Press, 1983).

Conclusion

An attempt was made to disentangle the various threads running through Mahatma Gandhi's relationship with Hinduism in terms of its characteristic institutions, its major scriptures and its primary thought patterns in the preceding pages. The time has now come to try to weave these threads together and to see if they form a coherent pattern when brought together. Perhaps a brief review of the facts each chapter brought us face to face with will help in forming an adequate judgement on this point.

When Mahatma Gandhi's relationship to the various sources of *dharma* was analysed, it became clear that for him the primary source of religious authority was the individual conscience rather than revealed scripture. He did not discard the role of scriptures and other sources of *dharma* but rather accorded primacy to conscience. Similarly, in dealing with the caste system he virtually reversed the caste hierarchy by upholding the rights of the *śūdras*, without again discarding the general architectonics of the system. In dealing with the stages of life or *āśramas*, Mahatma Gandhi shifted the emphasis away both from *gṛhastha* and *saṁnyāsa*, respectively favoured by the *pravṛtti* and *nivṛtti* orientations within Hinduism but rather espoused *vānaprastha*, without doing away with the other stages of life. His understanding of the *Rāmāyaṇa* and the

Mahābhārata — and specially the *Bhagavad-Gītā*, emphasized universal over particularistic ethics, a process which finds its full expression in his tendency to prefer *sādhāraṇa dharma* over *viśeṣa dharma*.

Perhaps all these conclusions can be reduced to the insight that *Mahatma Gandhi brought about cardinal changes within Hinduism by making ordinal changes within it*, thus resolving the paradox of *belonging* to a tradition, which he also himself *transformed* in the process of following it.

Bibliography

Bowes, Pratima, 1978, *The Hindu Religious Tradition*, London: Routledge and Kegan Paul.

Bridgewater, William and Hurtz, Seymour, eds., 1950, *The Columbia Encyclopaedia*, New York: Columbia University Press.

Bondurant, Joan V., 1958, *Conquest of Violence: The Gandhian Philosophy of Conflict*, Princeton, New Jersey: Princeton University Press.

Bühler, G., 1964, *The Laws of Manu*, Delhi: Motilal Banarsidas.

Chamber's Encyclopaedia, 1966, under Gandhi, Mohandas Karamchand, Oxford: Pergamon Press Ltd.

Chatterjee, Margaret, 1983, *Gandhi's Religious Thought*, London: The Macmillan Press.

Crooke, W., 1919, "Hinduism" in James Hastings, ed., *Encyclopaedia of Religion and Ethics*, New York: Charles Scribner's Sons.

Dasgupta, Surendranath, 1952, *A History of Indian Philosophy*, vol. II, Cambridge: Cambridge University Press.

de Bary, Wm. Theodore, ed., 1958, *Sources of Indian Tradition*, New York: Columbia University Press.

Desai, Mahadeva, 1956, *The Gita According to Gandhi*, Ahmedabad: Navajivan Publishing House.

Durant, Will, 1930, *The Case for India*, New York: Simon and Shuster.

Eggling, H. Julius, 1951, "Hinduism," in *Encyclopaedia Britannica*, Cromwell, Collier and Macmillan Inc.

Elder, Joseph W., 1966, "Hinduism," in *Collier's Encyclopaedia*, Cromwell, Collier and Macmillan Inc.

———, *Collier's Encyclopaedia* under Gandhi, Mohandas Karamchand, 1966, U.S.A., Cromwell Collier and Macmillan Inc.

———, 1970, *Chapters in Indian Civilization*, vol. I, Iowa: Kendall/Hunt Publishing Co.

Embree, Ainslie T., ed., 1972, *The Hindu Tradition*, New York: Vintage Books.

Encyclopaedia Americana, 1965 under Gandhi, Mohandas Karamchand, New York: Americana Corporation.

Encyclopaedia Britannica, 1968 under Gandhi, Mohandas Karamchand, U.S.A., Encyclopaedia Britannica Inc.

———, The New, (Macropaedia), 1974 under Gandhi, Mohandas Karamchand, Chicago: Encyclopaedia Britannica Inc.

———, The New, (Micropaedia), 1974 under Gandhi, Mohandas Karamchand, Chicago: Encyclopedia Britannica Inc.

Erikson, Erik H., 1970, *Gandhi's Truth*, New York: W.W. Norton & Co.

Everyman's Encyclopaedia, 1957 under Gandhi, Mohandas Karamchand, London: J.M. Dent & Sons Ltd.

Fischer, L., 1950, *The Life of Mahatma Gandhi,* New York: Harper & Brothers.

Funk & Wagnalls, *Standard Reference Encyclopaedia,* 1959 under Gandhi, Mohandas Karamchand, New York: Standard Reference Works Publishing Company Inc.

Gandhi, M.K., 1948, *The Story of My Experiments with Truth,* Washington D.C.: Public Affairs Press.

———, 1958, *Hindu Dharma,* Ahmedabad: Navajivan Publishing House.

Ghurye, G.S., 1969, *Caste and Race in India,* Bombay: Popular Prakashan.

Gonda, J., 1965, *Change and Continuity in Indian Religion,* The Hague: Mouton.

Gruzalski, Bart, 2001, *On Gandhi,* Belmont, CA: Wadsworth/Thompson Learning, Inc.

Herman, A.L., 1973, *The Bhagavad Gita: A Translation and Critical Commentary,* Springfield: Charles C. Thomas.

Hill, Douglas, W.P., 1928, *The Bhagavadgita,* London: Oxford University Press.

Hinnells, John R., and Sharpe, Eric J., 1972, *Hinduism,* Newcastle upon Tyne: Oriel Press.

Hopkins, Thomas J., 1971, *The Hindu Religious Tradition,* Belmont, California: Dickenson Publishing Company, Inc.

Iyer, Raghavan N., 1973, *The Moral and Political Thought of Mahatma Gandhi*, New York: Oxford University Press.

Jha, Ganganath, 1924, *Manu-Smriti Notes*, Part II, Calcutta: University of Calcutta.

Jordens, J.T.F., 1998, *Gandhi's Religion: A Homespun Shawl*, London: The Macmillan Company.

Kaji, Chhaganlal, G., 1909, *Philosophy of the Bhagavad Gita: An Exposition*, Rajkot.

Kane, P.V., 1962, *History of Dharmaśāstra*, vol. V, part II, Poona: Bhandarkar Oriental Research Institute.

———, 1968, *History of Dharmaśāstra*, vol. I part I, Poona: Bhandarkar Oriental Research Institute.

Mahadevan, T.M.P., 1960, *Outlines of Hinduism*, Bombay: Chetana Ltd.

Majumdar, R.C., ed., 1957, *The Vedic Age*, London: George Allen & Unwin Ltd.

———, ed., 1968, *The Age of Imperial Unity*, Bombay: Bharatiya Vidya Bhavan.

———, ed., 1969, *Struggle for Freedom*, Bombay: Bharatiya Vidya Bhavan.

Marshall, Roderick, 1965, "Hinduism," in *Encyclopaedia Americana*, New York: Americana Corporation.

Mehta, Ved, 1976, *New Yorker*, May 10.

Monier-Williams, Monier, 1976, *A Sanskrit-English Dictionary*, Oxford: Clarendon Press.

Moore, Charles, A., ed., 1967, *The Indian Mind*, Honolulu: University of Hawaii Press.

Moore, Charles A., and Radhakrishnan, Sarvepelli, eds., 1957, *A Source Book in Indian Philosophy*, Princeton, New Jersey: Princeton University Press.

Morgan, Kenneth, W., ed., 1953, *The Religion of the Hindus*, New York: The Ronald Press Company.

Muni, Jina Vinaya, ed., 1946, *The Jains in the History of Indian Literature by Dr. Maurice Winternitz*, Ahmedabad: Jaina Sahitya Samsodhaka Pratisthan.

Murty, K. Satchidananda, 1959, *Revelation and Reason in Advaita Vedanta*, New York: Columbia University Press.

Panda, K.B., 1974, *Sanatan Dharma and Law*, Cuttack: Mrs. Sushina Panda.

Pansikar, Wasudeva Laxmana Shastri, ed., 1912, *Śrīmadbhagavadgītā with the commentaries Śrīmat-śāṅkarabhāṣya with Ānandagiri; Nīlakaṇṭhī; Bhāṣyot-karṣadīpīkā of Dhanapati; Śrīdharī; Gītā-rthasaṁgraha of Abhinavaguptācārya and Gūḍhā-rthadīpīkā of Madhusūdana with Gūḍhārthatattvāloka of Śrīdharma-dattaśarmā*, Bombay: Nirnayasagar Press.

Payne, Robert, 1969, *The Life and Death of Mahatma Gandhi*, New York: E.P. Dutton.

Radhakrishnan, S., 1949, *The Bhagavadgita*, London: George Allen and Unwin Ltd.

Raju, P.T., 1971, *The Philosophical Traditions of India*, University of Pittsburgh Press.

Roy, S.C., 1941, *The Bhagavadgītā and Modern Scholarship*, London: Luzac & Co.

Sastrigal, K.S. Ramaswamy, 1927, *The Bhagavadgita with Translation and Notes*, Srirangam: Sri Vani Vilas Press.

Singer, Milton, ed., 1959, *Traditional India: Structure and Change*, Philadelphia: The American Folklore Society.

Smart, Ninian, 1970, "Hinduism," in S.G.F. Brandon, ed., *A Dictionary of Comparative Religion*, New York: Charles Scribner's Sons.

Spear, Percival, ed., 1958, *The Oxford History of India*, Oxford: Clarendon Press.

Srinivas, M.N., 1956, "A Note on Sanskritization and Westernization," *Far Eastern Quarterly*, vol. 15, no. 4 (August).

———, 1961, "Hinduism," in *Encyclopaedia Britannica*, vol. 10, Chicago: William Benton.

———, and Shah, A.M., 1968, "Hinduism," in David L. Sills, ed., *International Encyclopaedia of the Social Sciences*, The Macmillan Co. and The Free Press.

Tendulkar, D.G., 1951, *Mahatma, Life of Mohandas Karamchand Gandhi*, Bombay: Vithalbhai K. Jhaveri and D.G. Tendulkar.

Tikekar, S.R., "Bibliography or technophilia?," in *Gandhi Marg* 21(4).

Walker, Benjamin, 1968, *The Hindu World*, vol. I, New York: Frederick A. Praeger.

Whitfield, Foy, ed., 1978, *Man's Religious Quest*, London: Croom Helm.

Winternitz, Maurice, 1933, *A History of Indian Literature*, vol. II, Calcutta: University of Calcutta.

Zaehner, R.C., 1966, *Hinduism*, Oxford: Oxford University Press.

Term Index

Author Index

Name Index

Subject Index